ISRAEL
GOD'S HEARTBEAT TO THE WORLD

Robin (Rochel) Arne

ISRAEL
GOD'S HEARTBEAT TO THE WORLD

ROBIN (ROCHEL) ARNE

Israel: God's Heartbeat to the World by Robin (Rochel) Arne
Copyright © 2024 by Robin Arne
All Rights Reserved.
ISBN: 978-1-59755-829-7

Published by: ADVANTAGE BOOKS™
                Orlando, FL
                www.advbookstore.com

All Rights Reserved. This book and parts thereof may not be reproduced in any form, stored in a retrieval system or transmitted in any form by any means (electronic, mechanical, photocopy, recording or otherwise) without prior written permission of the author, except as provided by United States of America copyright law.

Scripture taken from the HOLY BIBLE, NEW INTERNATIONAL VERSION®. Copyright© 1973, 1978, 1984 by International Bible Society. Used by permission of Tyndale House Publishing. All rights reserved.

Library of Congress Catalog Number: 20244940030

Name: Arne, Robin Rochel
Title: Israel: God's Heartbeat to the World
                  Robin Rochel Arne
                  Advantage Books, 2025
Identifiers: ISBN Paperback: 9781597558297
                  ISBN eBook: 9781597558372
Subjects: RELIGION: Christian Life Inspirational
                  Religion Biblical Studies - General

First Printing: January 2025
25 26 27 28 29 30 31   10 9 8 7 6 5 4 3 2 1

Acknowledgements

    My focal point has always been the Lord when I graft words to paper. The opportunity I have been given stands strong in the field of knowing where to learn. The Biblical stance I adhere to is for all who read my work to gain the greatest ability to know Christ as I do. He is the caretaker of my heart. In Him I gained the will to proceed in the form of standing on His behalf. There is no greater partner to know. It is with this purpose I capture the love of writing and place it forward to others. Jesus is the Waymaker for this to happen. I am blessed to know Him in a personal manner. He supports me more than any other and due to His heart being connected to mine we act as one in accordance with the Word of the Bible. I gain in His direct path of trust. Together we tie with a garnered ability to put work toward the truth of His being.

    Scripture guides my every thought process. Thankfully I have Christ as my support beam for all things good and true. He never fails me, nor does He cause me harm. In Him I am made viable to others to share who the support measure is tied to. I will always believe God is all-powerful. Therefore, I will not lose footing or cast away the ambition I am gifted to perform. The value is a commitment I enjoy. Due to God, I am given the trust of others who found my writing supportive to their person. God is the reason I administer to others. Because of His great manner I lead in the way of true honor. Never will I release the love of God to my heart for He is eternal, and I am His witness in the making. The Bible reads as a body of faith to the one who transcribes it within him. Look to Christ for the unity and you will establish your own truth to Him for He always abides to the seeker His presence. Goals are a sight of birthing He administers so read with hope and find the support of the Word alongside of this material. It will captivate your love to God, and you will gain knowledge for all time.

Robin (Rochel) Arne

Introduction

The material to this compounded hope is for man to learn the nature of Israel to the people of the world. God has a perfect plan to formulate the need of man to learn who He is and His character traits as God of all things good and right. God will honor the people of His nation and truth will prevail. The love of the Father is a plan put in motion when time began in the Middle East. This is the place where man came to know the Savior of the world. To the Israelite Jesus is a mystery. Why this is the case is due to the influence of Satan against the people of the Holy One. God is all-knowing and, in the future to come, He will come to rule over all mankind. No other being can stand as the Lord of all can do. The birth of Israel is what put an established honor on a people group vested to claim the bond of true hope toward their mission field. God will perfect the role of many, and truth will come into play at the time of the tribulation. The event known as the rapture will draw up the people who are in love with the King. This book will ordain to the heart who the Savior of the earth reflects. The time is not known although the season is ripe for this to transpire. We wait in support of one another knowing God serves all of mankind for the better of their hearts.

Leadership is found in Scripture and the beauty of the Word it contains. Evaluate the manner of your own commitment to God and learn where the best avenue is to take for eternal bliss and happiness. God will not delay or press too quickly although He will grant the willing a staple of livelihood in where He acknowledges the character and supports the one who is in His midst of life. Knowing the Savior is good harmony and wise unity. Gain the power of the Lord and feed your spirit His able minded trust. You will hear the voice of truth and know the Risen God of all is about to gain entry to the earth we reside on.

Robin (Rochel) Arne

Table of Contents

ACKNOWLEDGEMENTS 5

INTRODUCTION 7

1: GOD THE ALL-KNOWING BEING OF SIGHT IS A JUSTIFIED CARETAKER AND SUPPORT MEASURE. 11

2: THE NEED TO PROSPER COMES TO THE ONE WILLING TO OFFER HOPE AND A PATH TO MANY 43

3: GOD WILL DELIVER A WAY TO KNOW HIS NAMESAKE, JESUS OF NAZARETH 75

4: THE LAND OF ISRAEL IS NOT FOR OTHERS BUT FOR THE JEWISH NATION ITSELF 109

5: THE PEOPLE OF ISRAEL ARE A GIFT OF UNITY TO MANKIND 143

AUTHOR BIO 175

Robin (Rochel) Arne

Unity Marker One

God the All-knowing Being of Sight is a Justified Caretaker and Support Measure.

God the one who made heaven and earth is all-knowing and supportive to all mankind. He is more than just a Lord of hope for He entertains mankind and offers the love of Him forward to them. The value of the one who professes to love the Savior is a talent all its own. God operates with a purpose and in Him is the trust of many. Leading is what favors the heart where man is found in support of Christ. Jesus was born in the Middle East and He was acclaimed as righteous. To believe in the way He operated is to know Him with honor. Israel is the reason we know who the Lord is and what He acts as. God is not small in His reporting of the great way. The bounty of the Book of hope is based on Israel and its contents speak to the great way of the Lord. Our Risen Christ is the one who offered Himself toward the heart of all mankind. In Him is the value of the ideal witness. The ability of God to ordain the kinship of the people of Israel shows us who we are to Him in a personal way. He values those who support Him in care. Our outlook needs to accompany Him in the way of committed hope and unity. The perfect way to do this is to read Scripture and believe in the power it contains. The Almighty gave us the will to follow in faith when He grafted us in His image. The Bible relates this message, and we gain the understanding by applying the Word of hope to our minds and character.

So God created man in his own image, in the image of God he created him; male and female he created them. Genesis 1:27 NIV

Israel is the way to understand the Savior and His personality type. He crafted the nation to witness His way of being. We learn and gain from the profit of knowing the Word of Christ. The unity of God to this particular people group is a measure of His support and love to all. Knowing the value of Christ is a belief in where many found the love of Him valuable. The person willing to offer this unity to another is someone worthy of knowing on a personal level. If value is a measure of trust, there's no better offering than Christ. For He sacrificed His own stand to complete for mankind the way to know Him and His Father, the great One of faith. God is supportive of any who believe and invite Him into their spirit. The love God has for man is far reaching and good in all forms. He is tied to the one who places his heart in His hands with free abandonment. The unity is not a small undertaking for the witness is solid and glory is given in the process. The way to know if salvation has taken form within your heart is to declare God is the one who made all that is good and true. The leadership of God is all encompassed. With His direct means of acting all can be tied to Him for eternity. He does not play favorites, nevertheless, He does give His heart to the one in need. The door to the center of His person is the One who hung with purpose on the cross of redeeming blood. God alone is the one who could manage the death and still stand as holy with no loss or negative standing. Where the one who places his heart with the One of true hope stands the witness God is all supporting to His child. We, the people of the earth, are all God's children. Still there is a difference as to who will be embraced at the throne gate in heaven. God is the one to determine who enters through the pearly gates. He knows us in a personal way, and we can't hide any dark presence from His all-knowing aptitude. He is the way to eternal bliss so unite with His character and stand in a way of committed trust. You will benefit and see the true way of being.

 The love of the Father is all care and no hardship. To love how He operates is to be vested with His personal way of being. God is all encompassed and in Him is the gain and favor man needs to survive in a holy way. To evaluate the role of God is not a gift of unity as man is not able to perform such a feat. The manner of truth is a shield against the enemy and in Him is the way to proceed. Knowing the way to ordain a goal is a stand of sight Israel completed in the past. However, most people of Israel always put forward an entanglement of no value. Today they believe Jesus has not come to the earth yet, they administer the prophesies of the Word. Blindness set in when they rejected the truth as it was given. To allow the

Word to settle within your heart builds the information and makes it clear to the heart and mind. Israel needs to learn how to embrace the Scriptures of hope and find the unity of God to them. They are willing to learn some of the Word except refuse most of the what the prophesy side has to offer. This is due to a lie told when Jesus arose from the grave.

> *⁵ The angel said to the women, "Do not be afraid, for I know you are looking for Jesus, who was crucified. ⁶ He is not here; he has risen, just as he said. Come and see the place where he lay. ⁷ Then go quickly and tell his disciples: 'He has risen from the dead and is going ahead of you into Galilee. There you will see him.' Now I have told you."*
>
> *⁸ So the women hurried away from the tomb, afraid yet filled with joy, and ran to tell his disciples. ⁹ Suddenly Jesus met them. "Greetings," he said. They came to him, clasped his feet and worshipped him. ¹⁰ Then Jesus said to them, "Do not be afraid. Go and tell my brothers to go to Galilee; there they will see me."*
>
> *¹¹ While the women were on their way, some of the guards went into the city and reported to the chief priests everything that happened. ¹² When the chief priests met with the elders and devised a plan. They gave the soldiers a large sum of money, ¹³ telling them, "You are to say, 'His disciples came during the night and stole him away while we were asleep.' ¹⁴ If this report gets to the governor, we will satisfy him and keep you out of trouble." ¹⁵ So the soldiers took the money and did as they were instructed. And this story has been widely circulated among the Jews to this very day. Matthew 28:5-15 NIV*

The people of the day were a tired and unholy group of people. In their manner was a selfish way not tied to Christ but their own way of being. The value to God was not written on the tablet of their hearts. Leading was a single endeavor and most pursued the knowledge of others over that of the written Word of a prophet. To know the Word but to act according to one's own selfish way is not a stand of insight but rather that of a lost soul. God is perfect in His decision making. He led with hope and true honor, except mankind favored the lie of self-imprisonment. Satan is crafty and the alure of him causes man to cast a shadow to the true nature of saving one's ability to know God. The lead of any who put forward the lie he need only to have self-control, and great things can happen falls victim to the understanding of deceptive goal making. The embellishment of the law was how man operated in the day of Israel's first undertaking. God scattered the people due to unbelief but now they reside in the promised land due to God's forgiving nature. He will call them to Him, and truth will prevail. It will take drastic measures for this gift to come before them although in the end, all will call upon Jesus for salvation.

The love of the Father is all-knowing and in Him is the found unity man desires to have. The evaluation of reading Scripture points to the realm of authority known as Christ Almighty. The value of the One you pursue cannot be obtained by merely belief alone but that of applying the heart toward His person. To evaluate the leading as righteous and holy one must first have the faith of a child. To quote the Living Word even the demons believe except they are not committed to serving the one true Author of man.

^{18} But someone will say, "You have faith; I have deeds." Show me your faith without deeds, and I will show you my faith by what I do. ^{19} You believe there is one God. Good! Even the demons believe that- and shudder.

Knowing the Risen King is to have the value of Him within your heart. Accepting Him as all-powerful is to have the structure of true knowledge in where you can apply it to another. If you place your heart in the hand of Christ, you will draw near to Him in character. You won't evaluate a dream and stand without courage to make it happen. The unity will be present and in the making of the light will the prosperity reside. Goals of hope form and man unites to the region of trust God has given him. The lead of man to another is to place the trust in Christ Jesus as the main form of witnessing. You will gift another simply by being a sound character being in where sin does not reside. Yes, man will always have sin in him yet the one taking steps toward not acting out in this area will be the glorified character of trust leading to the value of God to mankind.

People yearn to know who planned the heavens and the earth. The One who did is known to man if he believes and professes the hope to himself. Jesus is the one who made these value systems. He and the Father were tied together and in them was the ability to deliver a place of beauty. Both God and His offered Savior are fed one to another with character and honor. To team with them is wise and good judgement. Leading to know the One who made you is a plan offered for all on planet earth. Everyone who needs true hope finds it when they invite Jesus into their hearts. The goal to climb a hill is hard at times if it is steep and abundant with rough terrain. God the Father leads where the least amount of difficulty is present. God is not a being of loss, rather the wise reason to offer support. Knowing God comes to the one who invests with the formation of true hope and faith. God supports the mind and the meaning of Him is favor to the heart. God is valued to the many who gained Him in a personal manner. The Holy Spirit guides and the character of His way is ever proportionate in that it never fails or loses value. To align with God is to support Him in the way of always being respondent to Him with unity. The King of the world is Christ. He came to the earth to free man so he could know Him and find unity to the Father. This is the value all of mankind needs to claim. If there is a tug within your spirit accept the Living God of Jesus and invite Him to claim you as His own. In the way of tying the favor to your heart a stand of unity will evolve, and trust will grow.

The unity of God is for all mankind and in Him is the way to live in a bright manner. Knowing the way to gift another the truth of Scripture means man can provide the unity to anyone willing to learn the value of Christ. Leadership is not a small inherit gift it's rather the bounty of knowing how to operate with a leading ability to gift many the role of sharing love and hope. To know the One who made mankind is a gift of insight leading to the well of hope known as Scripture. The Bible is complete when both the New and Old Testament are witnessed. The unity it offers is a gain in where all people find the value of it and subscribe to its intellect. God has given man the ability to know Him in a personal way. We should work to know how to grant ourselves the light of the King. Reading the Book of true knowledge is a stand necessary to gain the support of the Creator. To understand the well front of faith one must apply his heart and mind to the study and gain the instruction of truth. The way we tie our hearts and minds toward God is what determines the value we hold to Him. His character is sound and because He cares for His people, we are fed hope and unity. Trust in God is representative to whom we support. The value of the One designing the unity is a value you can't place a dollar commitment on. It is a gift by profession and acceptance of His counsel. The Holy Spirit is our guidance professional, and He never fails in His offering. God elects the people who are willing to conquer the doubt and saddle up to Him in love and harmony. He places the truth of Him before their hearts and minds to evolve them into His care. He is always prospering many so be a part of the people group who lead with character. You will find unity supports your inherit knowledge and true hope will ensue. The downcast find the avenue to share and know God simply by expressing the honor of God forward. Love is a necessary stand we all need. It is a lonely place without the will of many in our lives. To have people who plan and commit to you says you are valued. The role of many finds a cove of planning and the goal builds with insight.

God will align the people of the Middle East and truth shall prevail. How He invests is clearly witnessed in the Scripture material of the Word of God. He has placed men in the position of caregiving so Israel will learn how to declare God the only one to bind with. The Father of the Word is God Almighty and He never forgets the important value He has on the people. In God stands the unity many look to find but know when it comes to favor Israel is always the apple of God's eye. Scripture teaches you to know the One who mastered the lead of many is to organize the spirit into future love and goal making. God has perfect timing, and He will show the many where He stands with character being forefront. God never loses so Israel will always be a part of the Mideastern way of livelihood. No other nation has been given the ability to fight when all the odds are against them. Because of the hand of protection God supplies Israel blossoms and progresses with hope. The unity of Christ has not been understood however that is going to change in a drastic way. God has not forgotten how to approach someone in the dark. The tribulation era will enlighten mankind as to the honest intent of God to witness to all generations. Any who have not put forth the true love of himself to Jesus will find a value missing on judgement day. Without the Living Word of God man is not able to perform with character or to gain in the many offered hopes of true support found in the hand of Christ. Only Jesus is the salvation bridge and in this understanding is the goal of knowing the One who made the people of the earth. The value of God is not small or less than for it is the only plan for eternal gain forever. God supports the one who believes in Him and who offers this gain to any in need. The unity of Christ is a stand of support necessary to allow for a better day ahead. In God is the benefit of knowing the leading of a true warrior of integrity. God values the way one ordains the mind in the character of Him. If you have the belief God might be who He claims to be you have the Holy Spirit knocking on your soul for admittance. Stand in the claim God has a Son and divest your heart toward the Caregiver of man. You will learn the manner of true hope and solid witness making will abound.

> *^{16} "For God so loved the world he gave his one and only Son, that whoever believes in him shall not perish but have eternal life. ^{17} For God did not send his Son into the world to condemn the world, but to save the world through him. ^{18} Whoever believes in him is not condemned, but whoever does not believe stands condemned already because he has not believed in the name of God's one and only Son. John 3:16-18 NIV*

The power and care of the life of man is not favored until God is accepted and made within him. This allows for the birth of unity to unfold. The total time it takes is seconds at best for God hears the love in a quick way. God never leaves one alone until they claimed Him as false and refused to follow Him in faith. Israel has operated as though there is no Christ, the Risen God of man. To believe in Christ is necessary for all of mankind to find prosperity and hope. The one who places his heart in the hand of God stands complete. There is a distinction between God the Father and Jesus, His Son. The value of both remains as a unity tied together in a holy matrimony. Many are willing to believe God exists, although few believe He is the Waymaker to the Father. The two mesh as a gift to mankind. There is only hope and value from on high. To evolve into the labor of knowing God supports your stand is to accept Him as the one who crafted you to begin with. The trust of knowing the One of hope is found by the application of gain due to love and honest trust. Jesus is not one to allow someone a unity until he has embraced Him as the one who hung at Calvary for his sins. The gift was done so all of man could reside with the Creator. To love and hope in the Master is to allow Him the prospect of serving you for all time. Yes,

God's influence is support. Never a diminished aptitude of loss for the sake of no knowledge. When the One who mastered your desire to gain forms a dream or invested idea know He will declare it forward and trust will be witnessed. Leading comes to the one who stands in the mirror of sight from God and believes He is working to control the outcome. God does not fail and in Him is the value of true honor.

God values the person who develops his way forward for the sake of knowing the Risen Lord of man. To allow God the ability to move freely within your heart is to grant Him the quest of serving others as well. The plan for another is not the need but the support of him gains one the fruit of insight. To place your mind in character to Christ is to evaluate His lead and offer it forth to the many. When there is an ability to share the work of your stand let God grant the way to move ahead. In Him is the unity of trust and it will encompass the whole idea not just a small portion. If you have the gift to learn, take the commitment and gift it forward. Sharing your heart with another in the way of true hope is to offer a pattern of intake negating the role of author as Jesus is the one who feeds the spirit. He not only detours the enemy from harming the plan He destroys his offered lie. God is supportive to the lead of His character so work as though the King is at your side knowing He is perfectly timing your future with capable hands. The love of Christ is a goal for anyone seeking to know Him better. If you value the unity to God, learn His way of operating and find the true nature of who He is. The Bible stands as the way to do this. Each page holds a benefit. You may need hearing of love or goal-making and in the process of declaring the Risen God is all-knowing you will gain the unity and be able to invest within the true Word of God. He builds character and He orchestrates the role of Him forward. Nearly every person who has ever seen the Scripture of life eternal has not forgotten it. This is due to its power. The voice of Christ is within the page material and glory to God is understood. Know the value of the pages and enlighten many as how to incorporate the term all-knowing forward. God can see and hear all the thoughts of every man. He does not fail to direct a person forward so opportunity can unleash the will of Him. If you see yourself as only an instrument used by the honorary God of man, you realized Jesus is the caretaker you need to operate in character. The value of man is great; however, it does not compare to the Risen King. He far surpasses any other being of inspiration. God supports the plan of knowing Him and leaning forward His makeup so don't feel as though your heart will not find favor in the work you do. All of man needs to be a stand of work ethic for trials to be accomplished. God rewards the one who invests forward for the sake of growing His kingdom. This means working for the sake of another has bearing. Even the janitor meets the necessary requirement to bend the heart of God. All are given the opportunity to shield someone in one form or another. How we operate in the way of true hope sets the standard of our daily output. The reverse pattern fails in its offering so develop the lead as righteous and good knowing you will carve out a better pathway for another. There is value to it and risen work will be achieved.

God is given to man to allow him a way to see clearly who made his character. If you value, the real committed way of offering hope you stand in a righteous way. God the Father is holy and true. In Him is the manner to know all things great and small. He never loses His way nor is He ever tempted to fail. He is just and good to the core. In Him is the support leading to a way of gain. It is for mankind Jesus hung and bled so witness His stand and declare Him your Savior. You will know Him in a personal manner and hope will ensue forth. Coming into the way of unity happens where faith resides. It takes the heart and mind declaring God supports them for unity to abide within. The need to stand on behalf of God will be your intent and you will share the knowledge when the doorway is apparent. To care for others and then take action to lead is a committed way of standing in favor. Allow God the ability to glean from you the way to speak and act in accordance with His love and character. The need to witness comes to the person willing to offer a way ahead to another. God is ever faithful to build with hope so invest in people and share the Gospel and light. You won't regret harvesting another for the sake of the kingdom. The One who plans for many to receive the light is God Himself. The saving power of Jesus is not a simple thing to be forgotten. All who heard the true Word of God know it stands as a message of faith and unity. God the Father never had a more glorious dream than for mankind to know Him in a personal manner. Jesus is the gateway for this to be achieved. God did not sacrifice His Son to cause Him harm or mistreatment. He enabled the whole of earth to have harmony with His heart. The way of true hope rests at Calvary upon the blood of the Lamb, Jesus Himself. Our light comes by way of determining the true gain of knowing the Risen One of favor. God is the way to offer another the needed bond of trust aligning with His character. The King is the way to survive for all time in trust and value of hope. Leading is for the Master's hand and in Him is the unity to thrive and gain by way of a witness to Him. If value is how you operate, knowing the Creator is the first step to trusting in His value. God is perfect in all He does. He never makes a mistake, so the people of God are His choice in the making. Israel is a people group we learn from. Their initiative is a stand we can invest toward. Leading forms where the light is present, and God has bestowed to them the value of His way. God has been the foundation of this region of hope and through His offering at Calvary many found Him forthright. He is the sight plan of solid knowledge where man supports and leads with character. Israel, today, is a small region with hope at its core. The stand of God is still within her. Leading in many areas of economics Israel is to be commended and revered. The maintenance of the work comes into play and by the leading of Christ the gateway to know Him is ever before their hearts and minds.

The Savior's leadership has always been for the people of the world to know Him better. Israel is an example of this truth. God has given mankind a people group to learn from. Since the beginning of time recorded knowledge has been presented. God has perfect knowledge and in Him is the stance of unity. The love and care from the Father to those who served in the Biblical era are found on the page material of the written Book of hope. Scripture is a value not accounted for without the due diligence of serving the work in prayer. If you read the account of hope without uniting to the One who masterfully made the contents, then you have not accepted the value as truth. God supports the reader with true insight and in the maintenance of seeing the value one aligns spiritually with character and true gain. To evolve in a ministry first look to God for the knowing aptitude of unity otherwise all you strive for will evaporate as there will be no real root taking shape. The more you learn about the nature of the King the more valuable Scripture is to you. The Book of Hope is found in many locations, only not all material is sound. Review the work before assuming it is right. How do you know how to choose the correct standard edition?

Acknowledge the One who made you then see where the truth of the Book aligns. Are there menus pointing to the Risen Jesus and is He credited with the saving of the spirit? Do the Scriptures you see look to offer hope for the one in need over that of true knowledge? Are there lies present not adhering to the preaching of true honor to the Savior? If the truth is what you are seeking, ask a witness who has offered the knowledge of a feast of insight. If today's values are put before you with no curtailing of honor, it is not of God. The world today embraces the lie of homosexuality. This is not Scripture based. Look at who made the current edition. Is it a practicing body of believers or is there a new name with no foundation to serve them? The knowledge of truth will convict the heart and cause it to stir regarding the value of Christ. He died for mankind to find the true way to know Him. Standing on the hope man can live in his own manner is to believe Christ is not who He claims to be. You can't have a true yearning of faith if you invest in the market of falsehood. To justify your own thought process is to lose sight of the committed partnership of God's care. Work for a stand of pure living and hope will be granted. God is the directive and in Him is the value system of light. He does not fail to know He is perfect, and He protects those who truly have Him as their wise counsel.

> *[24] Therefore God gave them over in the sinful desires of their hearts to sexual impurity for the degrading of their bodies with one another. [25] They exchanged the truth of God for a lie and worshipped and served created things rather than the Creator-who is forever praised. Amen.*

> *[26] Because of this, God gave them over to shameful lusts. Even their women exchanged natural relations for unnatural ones. [27] In the same way the men also abandoned natural relations with women and were inflamed with lusts for one another. Men committed indecent acts with other men and received in themselves the due penalty for their perversion. Romans 1:24-27 NIV*

Christ is the one who perfected the meaning of gifted hope. By His person man can be fed the true hope of knowing Him in a personal manner. This valuable read is found in Scripture where all are given the opportunity to bind with Jesus. The truth of the Word is for all mankind not just one individual or the brightest of men. Even the pauper can gain unity by simply believing and putting in motion faith. God is perfect and He never forgets a name or face. To believe in Him is wise and it grants the unity of prayer. To level off in a way of insight is to declare God the Risen Savior. Have the benefit of sight and lean toward the true hope of man. Jesus is the way to bloom in favor. The idea man is not who God adores is a false understanding. God created man to learn from Him and to gain in faith due to an abundant offering from on high. The value system of God is not something to let loose of. Knowing Him is the great way to thrive for all time. Trust is a favor applied into action. The Bible shows man how to operate and care for one another. Leading is standing in faith and support of others. The value of knowing the One who made you is far superior to having a bank account of riches. God is the one I lean into for all my goal making. It is by His power I am fed and supported. The unity of Him to my heart is never lost or without hope. I value Him as my whole being of trust. Let God be the one to deliver a sound presentation in where you verbalize the necessary output to others leading to growth in Christ. To permit God the ability to offer through your mind and heart the knowledge of His character is to gift Him your support. Trust builds where hope lies so lean toward the support of the King. You will be led to the stream of unity and grow with a knowledge God supports you as His child of favor.

    God's ability to provide for His people is that of true love and glorified honor. God is not a calling of doubt, rather that of true hope and support. We lead into favor by applying the idea God made man. Which opens the sight of knowledge. He is the great Creator. Christ is significant in He died at Calvary for the sins of all. God is the way to salvation, except it is Jesus who hung with purpose. The value cannot be measured or figured in the way of the usual study material. It takes the application of reading the Word of hope to find the witness of the King. God offered mankind the way to know Him in a personal manner. We have been given the knowledge of Christ. The Scriptures declare Him as good and forthright. The way to obtain wealth is to believe and stand in support of the one who made the way to heaven's door is an entrance we can gather to. The love of the Savior far surpasses any man's offering so believe and gain the light of unity. You won't be fooled by another as there is no power without the blood of Jesus and that is what the message of salvation is designed for. True hope is in the blood of the Lamb. He is the sacrament of true gain where all are welcome to establish a home front. Heaven is a place where all people hope to claim so lean forth to Christ and gain the advancement. You will see Him as faithful and righteous, not dark or intrusive. God values the role of author so tell your story and share your heart. It will reflect the value of God, and His people will be revived.

In the beginning God created the heavens and the earth. Genesis 1:1

God is all the world needs to thrive and be granted unity in favor. The one who maintains the lead of author grows in character and values the way of God. There are many ideas in the making, however, when God is at work real trust is conquered. God showered mankind with His wealth of goodness, but then man forgot Him and turned to his own way of being. This led to the death and burial of Christ. However, it was the gateway for all to find the passage of the claim of eternal life. God did not die alone or without others serving Him in value. The apostles cared deeply, and they too often had to share the burden of pain for witnessing on behalf of Jesus. To know the Risen God of all is to stand with Him in support. He values all of man, so you aren't without a following in the same manner. People across the world know God is who He claims to be. The Bible has supported many and in its pages is the way to find hope leading to prosperity of the heart. There is no other who can ordain the gift of salvation for all time. Jesus cares about all living creatures. He will stand holy and gain man the unity if one is willing to acquire the hope filled light. When there is a mechanism right fitted to allow one a better chance at claiming the way to gain accept it at face value and learn where the offering abides. When God granted His Son to mankind it was for the benefit of His name to be spread with support. The manner of death to man is that of a fallen world in where temptation has a foothold. The only way to combat the negative is to offer your heart and mind the true knowledge God is the only gateway to life. Death has no hold in where man is taken into the depth of darkness. Jesus is the light offering and to dine on His ability to save is to grant the heart the support necessary to produce a whole and complete life of worship. Leading is not of human nature in where truth is always the idea presented. There are many who have fallen victim to the value of knowing about a false implant. This is not God's way. In Him is the value of all things right and true. He never loses His character due to money or fame. For these are not what make Him drawn to the human race. God pursues mankind simply for the relationship side of the undertaking. He wants all people to experience His good character. To truly know the One who made you is to invest time in His cultured Book. It tallies the heart into the manner of knowing how to operate in good support. Never has there been a person unwilling to value the true nature of God if he witnesses the righteous way of Jesus. The only one who does not believe is the man who decided God is false and not real to His Word. This is deceptive for God is the one who made all things good and pure. Trust the Risen Waymaker and know He serves the man who trusts in Him for He loves the faithful and true servant.

Where the truth of the Word is fed to mankind true hope unfolds. God values all who administer for His namesake. The unity of Christ Jesus is for all who choose to believe and support the One who claimed man for Himself. God supports the love of many. To stand on behalf of another is to work so many can find the freedom of the great I Am. God the Father is recognized by the Jewish people. He has been steadfast in their faith. God supports the will of their being, yet they rejected Christ the Savior. As a result, many followed the deceptiveness of Satan and lost the true inheritance of the Risen King. Leading in the way of supports one must operate with insight. God does not hide His character, nor will He stand without unity to Him. Value to God means the acceptance of the One who made you. Jesus is the value system all of mankind needs to know. The gateway to God is through His Son, the Lord God of all. The inherit ability to thrive is based on the unity to God not the witness of mankind. The vital way God operates is to lead and embrace man as His own. God supports those who have the sight of Him as the lead of guiding stamina. True support is from on high not just the idea of Him but the whole intent He portrays needs to be understood. The unity of knowing the One who created you is a gift of knowledge standing in a righteous way. To visualize the lead and embrace the call gains one the true will of the saving power of God. Salvation is a plan from the One of true hope. He is the value system all of man needs to prosper. The ability to learn comes from reading the Book of faith. The record it offers is all good and harmonizing. There is none greater to learn from than the Master Himself, Jesus is His name! To align your heart in the direct path of God is to stand in support of the living Word. The Bible, complete with the Old and New Testament, is the way to have gain and trust. Knowing the way to learn is to be guided in unity by the Lord. Jesus never leads without hope so when you hear the call lean toward the plan He puts forward. Know the goal is within reach and you will have the trust necessary to ordain for another the trust you found. God is not one to simply adhere without purpose. In His value system is a bounty of true honor and commitment. Leading is a stand He operates from. Form a bond and let Him gift you with the trust to stand on His behalf. You will find unity and good harmony will abide.

To know the One who made man is to believe He is real and good. In the making of Scripture God tied mankind to His person. God reflects His character and in the value of Him comes the will of His demeaner. God supports the one willing to advance for the sake of others not just themselves. Leading is for the person who has a goal in where faith is necessary and true. God values the way man operates, and in His unity, man abides with support. The trust of Him is ever before your heart. What matters is whether you invite His counsel, or you reject it due to lack of insight. Reading the valuable work of the Bible is to declare God is who He claims to be. The fruit it gifts is for all who treasure God as their personal Savior. Jesus, the Messiah, is the Waymaker of hope. In His tally is the sight plan of the birth of a generation who pressed on in favor and followed Him is spirit. Outside of Israel is the committed region of America, the country of freedom and value to God. However, this is unique to the spirit of Christ in that the community is now gaining in the way of total realization He is about to appear. How do we evaluate this dream. Scripture points us to the knowledge God has perfect timing. Years ago, the nation of hope put forward the light and care of the Savior. Today many laws have been influenced by darkness and people have lost the truth and knowledge of God. Their hearts are no longer committed to the gain of insight found by applying truth to a daily regimen. The glory of God is not being given and man is false in his representation. Many now honor other ideas and they pressed for false narratives leading to no knowledge of the Caretaker. Our unity in God was once a gift of hope and committed yearning. Today man is ever detailing his own agenda. This has turned our nation into a loss of hope or forthright investment. God will not continue to lead us where He is not welcome. We could stand on behalf of the Word and its value making, however, we no longer put in play the way of Jesus in hopes of having our own understanding. Man leads and fails miserably. He is not capable of knowing the truth without the Word within him. False ideas form and man leans on his own value system which is not holy or true. Only the unity found in God is real and just. There is no better influence than the light of the King. He supports more fully how to behave and gain trust. His leading is valued above all there is to see or know. Take to heart God is close at hand as the world has crumbled in a severe loss of hope. God loves people and to Him each one is unique. He doesn't want to lose them to the falsehood of the enemy. He will protect the work of His manner, and the day of reckoning will come. It is a promise from on high! God stands as righteous and true. In Him is the unity man desires without fully knowing its true value. Accept the light and favor God supports and be a witness of truth. You will gain in the manner of support and a character stand will ensue. God knows the day and the hour of His coming. Be ready and invite Him into your life. You will hear Him speak and gain the voice of trust within you.

    The saving power of Christ is for all man to nourish others and lead them into eternal gain. How we apply our hearts and minds in the direct path of hope is what determines the value of the One who made all things good. God is unity in that with His character is the sight of trust bearing forward the knowledge He is good and holy. To believe the Savior is justified and true is to claim Him as the one who gifted the cure for sin nature. The level of commitment is found in the one who has captured another for the sake of glory to God. If you offered others the insight of knowing the one who made them, you have given forward the value of your salvation. God perfects the heart and leads it with character in that He never puts in motion a false graft. Leading comes to the one willing to ascribe forward a return, so others thrive and find care. God is the sight plan all need to believe so look at the Book of true hope and build so many find the trust and favor of the Most High. The general population cares little for the One who caretakes and grants livelihood. Knowing the sculpted gift of perfect love comes by way of invested trust toward Jesus and His claim on the heart. God permits man to choose his own way however there is a simple path to freedom if one secures the way to God. Knowing the Risen Savior is not something to push aside. It is the difference between safe for all eternity or ending in death and despair. God is the value all man needs to gain unity in the way of favor and light. Trust the One who made you and let Him design the element of your hope path. He will grant favor to the trust and worship will be the maintenance of gain. God is not one to offer Himself and let no opportunity ensue. He performs so better alignment happens and the heart builds with character for others to learn from. Allow the timing of God to be administered and you will savor the reward with a lead of standing.

God is the favorite to mankind when He is believed and honored by him. Faith is not seen where no action is put in play. The unity of knowing where to align is a sight of birthing needed to witness the true hope filled, love language of man to Christ. The witness of true love is the offered favor from the perspective of the faithful. God is perfect and true. He does not offer a false initiative in where no value is captured. When the heart places God in front of all else great knowledge unfolds. Reading the Bible is wise and honor forms toward Jesus. The true way to believe is to offer the work of your joy to that of God given options and in so doing a gateway will align. If you value time and enjoy reading hope filled truth, the Bible offers the best of these none can compare to. The knowing has the realization God is present upon the page material and in Him is the sound support leading to a future of hope. The unity of Christ to mankind has been offered since the birth in the manger. God supports the one who places his heart in the palm of Christ. There is no better gift than to know the One who made the stars and the planets. When one delivers the fact of this truth a whole support field is built. Whether you believe or have the idea within you a bond is being implemented. Reach toward the manner of insight and dine on the true hope of man. It is not weak but rather a holding of unity is standing with action as its backdrop. Those that know find the trust and act in accordance with it. If you have a bank account that reaches into the path of wealth, you have been given support. It may have taken you time to build this holding, yet God favored your effort and granted you the means to gain.

Why is there a difference in someone's wealth? Only God can answer the reason but to serve Him in faith is a balance of insight none can compare to.

The world is clever in its own way of thinking. The One who made heaven and earth knows the detail of the sun not just its look and heat. God is the crafter who witnessed the moon in plain view to mankind. He created the goal of knowing how to fly and where to align the spirit with true unity. In Him is the value none can compare to. The perfect unity of Christ to mankind is found in the reading of Scripture. It is far more valuable than any offered insight outside of the true Book of knowledge. God is not one to ordain the mind into a loss or a misguiding in that all he cares for He invests toward. God can make a wise goal possible where no other can apply the witness to bend the heart of man. To know the One who made you is a talent and offered insight only God maintains. Knowing where to offer this unity is placed forth by the hand of Christ. The love of the Father is for man to know Him and His ordination of truth. The goal to give many the hope of God is a significant idea and one that requires the path of leading to be made right and glory giving. God receives the offered plan and forms it to a wise growth in where many have the witness of trust and gifted insight. If time has evaporated, and there is no stand to offer a forthright objective you may have been under the influence of the deceiver. Know God can build anything He decides is of importance to Him. It may require a plan of action you aren't finding illuminating although within the goal a definite feed will come forth. To love the Risen One who made all you have is to place your value on Him and not the unity to an object or being outside of God, Himself. God values the leading you entered on His behalf. Trust Him to stand in the way of true hope and look to His manner for guiding. You will not fail where hope resides, and you will know the One of man in a personal way. God delights in the spoken Word of truth. He will grant you an idea and make it clearly obtainable when the time is precise. Know you're not a witness without hope when you work on behalf of Him with courage and idea building. God knows the role of faith and in Him is the way to prosper. Believe He offers the value needed to address the bounty and declare it good. He never offers a less than good alternative.

In the beginning was the Word, and the Word was with God, and the Word was God. John 1:1 NIV

The love of man is not as the love of the Lord. Through the generations recorded in the written Scriptures we see man fails in comparison. The Creator is righteous and good where man needs support to work as a mentor of goodness. We have many ways to share today with technology yet, few are crying out who is the Living Word. It takes a preparedness of work for others to learn about the great I Am. He is unique and set apart. None can compare to the righteous God of the universe. Knowing the One who made you is insight at its finest. Leading is a gift and in the motion one can bridge the gap between a small talent and one of hope filled insight. Love from on high is a graft to the One who stands complete in where man needs others to help aid in his walk of life. We work as a team when building for the same purpose, yet Christ can do anything He desires as He is always correct, and unity is all He knows. The Father and Jesus are team members but also joined as one body. How this is we can only imagine. God ordained Himself to be separate but also one. We can argue about many differences, however this fact remains standing. To separate one from the other loses the true witness found at Calvary. The cross is an emblem of favor we find supporting our hearts and minds. When one gifts another the understanding Jesus is the King of the Jews a realization takes form. Not all countries embrace the Christ of love and in the loss, laws ensue that damage the outreach simply because false understandings fill the void.

The One who made mankind is not a planner of destruction. In God is the will to live and blossom with character. Religion is not the voice of Jesus. In Him is the unity to offer the love He shared upon His death and resurrection. It is deep and it withstands all time. If He were not who He claims to be He would have dissipated long ago in the mind of man. God overruns the negative with light and true hope. Those that know will offer the light and stand where others fear. Even the slim chance of finding favor means man can know the One who made him. God is light and true patronage to mankind. He invests in character and provides the love of Himself to engage with each person freely with hope. Depression comes to the manner of one who does not believe or apply faith to Christ. The walk is slight and does not bear fruit in where one who believes and accepts the hope finds the precious life of God to be fulfilling. Things of old pass away and the new replace the dire will to that of trust and insight leading to character and a forthright objective. God is skilled and makes a way for many to find the value of Him as their own manager. Light offers man the knowing way of Christ. Whether he receives it or leaves it aside depends on his willingness to hear the reward of true value. God is perfect and in Him is the guidance of true acknowledgement. Leading comes to the one who believes and maintains the connection. It will flourish where it is fed. It takes the application of reading the unity binder. Both the Old and New Testament are what matches the mind to the call and favor of the Most High. Embrace the vision of God and be reconciled to Him with glue of faith. In the battle of knowing the One of light comes the gift of understanding. It takes the gain of a mustard seed to accomplish this act.

> *"He replied, "Because you have so little faith. I tell you the truth, if you have faith as small as a mustard seed, you can say to this mountain, 'Move from here to there and it will move. Nothing will be impossible for you. Matthew 17:20 NIV*

God is the way to know hope for all time. In Him is the balance of receiving true honor and glory for His person. God does not get prideful, nor does He offer a false narrative. It is His manner to offer a plan of salvation fit for a king. Only in Him is man found holy or good. Without the saving power of Jesus's blood no one would have the ability to prosper or move in harmony to God. He never loses His advancement when a subject is being put forth. It may require a fruit filled endeavor or a time of waiting only know the solid manner is found in Christ's lead. To offer man the knowledge you learned is to point him to the One who made all things right. God never loses His investment for He can withstand the wait of time required for the whole endeavor to be made good. Man likes a quick return but then when the saving power is enlisted there may reside timing to come into play. Belief is a factor requiring action. Plan for the goal to be forthright and true by offering your best intent toward the project. In the Lord is the way to find favor due to the abundant, holy admission God is faithful. When the work is being invested and no return is at hand believe God is moving where you are not able to witness. Spiritual guiding needs the developed way of unity for progress to ensue. Allow the One of unity to perfect your idea making and stand in character to His person. You will reside in the care of the Most High and in the making will be the witness of His love. God is the one who withstood a desperate situation and still came out victorious. The day of reconning is at hand so plan for unity at this hour. Don't wait for the next tug at your heart as you don't know the final attempt and when it will be there. In the scope of reading the Word look at how God operated with the Israelites. He showed them the trust and offered the way of Jesus yet, there were the deceptive workers who spread lies about the grave being empty. As a result, man has not believed in the Jewish community.

A. simple developed hope can spring into action the full, involved way of knowing the Savior so let freedom come and accept God's favor in a freewill sight plan. You will hear the spoken trust and be dining on the capital of a wise being of a gifted unity no other is able to provide.

Jesus did not die so man would be left with no hope. Because He cared and desired to create harmony for man to Him the cross was a necessity. The love shown on Calvary was all true and good in where man found the truth of Scripture fulfilled. The people who search for the truth of the Word find the unity it provides, and they invest in the knowledge with abandonment. God performed a miracle that day and all who believe are standing in character to His person. To maintain God as the spirit of faith is to have the unity of a guiding hope. The Holy Spirit will engage where He is welcomed and that happens upon the admission of Jesus as the one, true King He claims to be. King of the Jews was recorded upon the head of the cross. Though it was placed there as a mocking stand, in truth it was the witness of holy trust. To know God is to understand Him as the ruler with a caregiving aptitude. The level of prosperity leading to a value of favor is the real unity found in the Word. The whole Bible is the truth of righteous love. God is perfect and in Him is the sight birth of a redeeming Savior. The One who made mankind is the same God of today. He hasn't changed nor will He ever. For He is made of pure hope and in His character stands the righteous grant of forever. Heaven is a dream to all who believe there is life eternal. Knowing the way to gain this plan is to align with the One who made you from dust. Each particle is not wasted nor is it of little bearing. God is the Crafter all of us look toward as righteous. Even the unbelief serves a purpose. It speaks to the often-lost man in need of salvation. Knowing God is a value none can compare with so dine on His person and pray to be a witness who recognizes the value of Him so others can find the unity as well. Love from on high is a stand of insight the saved learn by. Accept the Word and the character of the One who granted man the ability to find His support from the blood of atonement. The walk-in faith will be a cascade of fruit and in the way of trust all will shine forward.

The manner of favor man supports need not be that of no effort of hope. In the way of tying to the One who made all things good is to declare Jesus is the way to life eternal. The Bible records the path of the many who found this unity and understood how to offer the light toward another. The people of the world were not without a lead in the day of the written Scriptures. It was a recording of how to stand and where to place the hope of man to God. The power from Christ came down from above and man found the unity solid and true. If you have not witnessed the love of Christ, it is not due to God not aligning Himself to your heart. It is simply that of the rejection you tossed His way. The love of saving another for the righteous call to God is a support beam all see as right. The person willing to administer the faith is someone who believes the stand of Scripture is a sure thing against the enemy of God. To battle without learning the Word is to believe you are stronger than Satan which no man is on his own. It takes the practice of faith and unity to God to be able to withstand temptation and the push from the enemy against your heart. Glory is given when man believes in the care and the love of God to him. God is all-knowing so He never learns after the fact. By spreading the Gospel message man has shown fruit to others. The way of seeding the flower bed is to plan and wait for God to nourish the ground so it can thrive and prosper. God loves all people. There is no other more precious to God than His created human beings. Even the animals of the earth aren't valued as highly. Scripture teaches man is made in the image of God. We have a special unity to Him that is more than just influence. He invests in our care and through the love He offers we are fed and supported with gain. He does, however, acknowledge us and our offered trust. If you fail to believe and only push away His offering, you will not be standing in favor but outside of it. The support of the Risen Lord is for man to know Him and truly care for His way of being. May believe they can operate without God's guiding insight. When this happens, man falls victim to a stand of no goal making. He will just build for the sake of unity to himself and all he strives for will wash away at judgment time.

    Jesus never intended for man to be alone. Through Him all of mankind is fed unity and true hope. In the power of Calvary where Christ died and rose from the dead leading ensued. How can this be? God cared for His people of Israel and He desired for them to learn who He was and what He was about. Even though God worked with mankind man favored his own idea making. Jesus bore the witness of a shared unity as the blood of redeeming power was shed. God is favor to mankind. Whether you acknowledge this truth or toss it to the wind does not change the fact it is real and right. However, if you reject the love God brought to mankind you are dammed for eternity. God does not look to man for a better way for He is the great Waymaker. In Him is the solid aptitude of a shared witness so man can thrive and prosper. God is all-knowing and He plans for a righteous way to be given to the one who stands on His behalf. Does this mean God is not all-consumed? No, for He can do all things right and good. He does not need another to lay claim to a goal He has set in motion. To love God with an abandonment is to trust in Him for your resource lead. He supplies the love of His spirit and in doing so many find the value of Jesus a gift not replaceable. Allow the importance to be standing within your heart and lean into the value of God not just the Father but the Son as well. To look to the One who cared enough to suffer, and die is to believe in His great way. Suffering is not a way to align with Christ as He paid the price in full for man to have eternal hope. The lead of Jesus is for all of mankind to know His favor. He stands in harmony with any who profess their hope in Him. With the goal of knowing where to grant others the love of God comes the beauty of a witness preparing the path of intent. The value of Scripture coordinates the lead and makes it cemented with truth. The unity of knowing where to find the character of God is a step-in faith and hope. A forthright aptitude is one of a managed insight found in caregiving to God. The hope of the Creator comes into play where man finds the trust and applies it forward. God is all-knowing and in Him is the understanding of who is willing to align their heart to His person. It takes the heart to connect with a righteous love not just a quick idea or thought but one of true intent with character and standing.

The value of God is for man to discover by reading the Old and New Testament. The whole Book of hope is solid and true. In the making of unity to mankind God offers Himself and He provides the plan to know Him better. The lead of something must be that of truth or why have the incentive to pursue the written idea? God is the character man needs to believe and to gain in the unity to Him. Trust is what cements the need and grows it with love. God is all-knowing. He does not fail, nor does He offer a false pretense so to gift someone the knowledge of the Scripture Book is to grant another the ability to thrive and hold fast to the One who made him live. The breath of life is not something simple or misguided where food for the heart is valued. God is the one who maintains the heart and leads it forth with character. In Him is the wise merit of trust leading to a witness of hope no other can provide. If God is the one, you believe in for aid you will aspire to offer others His way of being. The capital of one's stand is what we see as righteous or slim. God is unity and harmony. In Him is the support needed to grant the mind the true nature of His counsel. Leading is not simplistic where truth is given. Due to the number of authors who transcribe the Scripture Book there have been errors made still the stand of the Bible is complete. Should this worry the reader? Investigation sets the mind at ease. Know if there is a falsehood it will stir the spirit, and you will acknowledge something is not quite represented correctly. You can perform a goal of research and be among the faith bearing in short order. Bibles of the current writing period often are not hard to understand, as renditions have been made to clarify for man what the early language represented. Some, however, have been changed so much they no longer hold the value of light so when you apply your heart and mind look to the Word with character. If God is shown in poor lighting it is not Scripturally sound. God is perfect and true. He does not fail in His way of being. He is always light and good. Should you have questions, look to where your heart finds the support of a wise intention. Men will speak out of turn simply to gain the world yet someone who professes the light will speak out for the sake of saving the individual in need. A false lead will only take what God made right and change it to benefit their own manner. Faith is a requirement when learning is in motion. Know God does not differentiate from the point of view that all mankind is valued by Him.

Jesus is the gateway to life eternal due to His redeeming blood. Every drop was a gift we should never forget nor look at as a onetime deal. It is for all of mankind to gain by. Freedom from the sacrifices of the past is what transpired. Man needs a valued way to express his support to the One who made him. Jesus is that answer. In the care of God to man we are gifted the wellhouse of salvation leading us to the cross of eternal witnessing. God is perfect and true. He never fails or loses His ability to speak to our hearts and minds. His character is for anyone looking to be united in the way of forever. Hope is solid and unity is a gift. God supports the one who believes and offers himself to the love of God.

Scripture assures us Jesus has a record of His birth and lineage. There is no question God created all of mankind so why should we believe He doesn't know how to grant us His pure way of being? A bond of hope is all we aspire toward when light is what we seek. Jesus is the gold to mankind. He is perfect with character and in Him is the offered unity needed to claim righteous caregiving. A person who has committed the act of profession Jesus is Lord and Savior finds the faith necessary to apply this knowledge to many. God is not weak; He has chosen His people to share in the light and the recognized favor. It is a special unity when man believes enough to speak up for the One who crafted Him in a public manner. Knowing the role of trust plays an important lead is a grant of favor we are blessed to gain. The value of God is not something we can comprehend as He is too vast and great for us to fully know Him. He is more than any man and we need His counsel as our own to live with character and gain.

But the Counselor, the Holy Spirit, whom the Father will send in my name, will teach you all things and will remind you of everything I said to you. John 14:26 NIV

The love of the One who made all things good is always investing in people and their way of being when it is tied to Him personally. God supports the life of man and in the manner of favor He does not forget the many who honored Him with love. If you value, the Risen King and believe He is at work on your behalf. In Him is the ability to stand and create where others are not gifted. God values the person who freely gives his heart to Him. The love of God is not a small endowment, rather that of pure leading.

God is all-encompassing. He can perform a miracle and in doing so glorify Himself in such a way that no pride sets within His character. Man does not have that ability. We must tame our own unity as we feel compelled to look for honor and feeding. Our hearts have a sin nature, and we must stand against the draw of self-alignment. The operating manner of God is for man to have the unity that means growth in the way of spiritual leading. God is the value of our mind and knowledge. If you apply your actions toward Him for the good of another there resides the dream of outreach within your heart. God is all-knowing so He can always maintain the proper way to be. In the righteous way He blends our thought process to His is a gift of unity necessary to thrive. God is what we all desire even when we don't' understand we do. People through the generations longed for the glorious appearance of the One of faith. Soon this prophecy will happen. It may not be in our lifetime, yet it will take form. God is the craft builder who never fails. Time is not the same value to God it is to us. We need action to feel maintained yet, where God offers us building ability comes the goal of offering the right and good way. This can be difficult to withstand when we dream of a new way to grow. God's process is always that of true garnering. In Him is the support we favor. The love and care supplied by Jesus cannot be equated to any other thing. God is great at what He does so know He will offer you a program in where you align to Him and have the faith necessary to offer others the learning you have gained. He is a spiritual being with character. Blessed be His name!

    God's role is to level the playing field so many are given the hope He has to offer. Leadership is a value none has until God projects it to his heart. Love comes to the plan where man has the unity and believes God is a good caretaker. Knowing God is not a quest, rather that of acceptance. In God is the sight of hope leading to a galvanized way of being upright. You will reflect the Scriptures, and in the witness, true love will reign. God the Father is the doorway to heaven, still one must place his faith in the palm of Jesus to be secure. Knowing the love of God is felt in every breath of a baby. He incorporates the love He holds to the spirit and hope ensues. God is the one who has the ordination of faith, and He offers it forward to anyone in need. It takes little for man to invite in the Savior and His good way. A profession is needed so invite God into you with care and know He is ever worthy to be praised. God is honor to the quick of Him. He is not a gesture of no hope for He alone is the one who made the gift. God is true to His word, and He will show you His gain when you believe and accept Him as the Savior of the world. Doors are significant when growth is occurring. The leading of the One who made you is a spiritual being and in the manner of faith He is justified. To know the way to operate due to reading the verses of the Bible is to acknowledge God above all else. In doing so you offer the lead of a saved interest to others. The time challenge plays a part so don't wait with hopes of spreading unity. Act with respect and know God has heard you with His personal way of acknowledgement. He will not fail to support you with confidence and unity will abound. God offers all His intent of hope. There are those who found this an available work with no hardship of loss. Some, however, deem it too hard to follow another even when the light has shown them the way. God does not stand against the individual unwilling to offer himself to Christ. He waits with an open doorway and requests yet again for the plan of salvation to take root. But there does come a point where the rejection is too intended, and the loss remains for all time. This is the passage of no return. No man knows at what point this happens, so it is better to invite God within as soon as you esteem Him to be fruitful.

God the Father is all-knowing and in Him is the fruit of wealth all of mankind is in need of. His value far surpasses that of just hope. He is fed with His own ability. None have the same character as He and all try to gain in the way of Him. I have the worth of the way due to the hope He has given me. The value to prosper is for any who have the work of God as their own makeup. God is all things right and good. If man is not willing to learn of Jesus, no value is recorded. In Him is the avenue of favor all need to achieve the reward of hope. I know I am with courage and insight because Jesus is the one who prospered me in this way. I have taken the work I was gifted at and applied it to others in where the faith is a plan of support. No other feeds me with the support due to no gain of hope for man cannot provide another with a spiritual gift. This comes by way of Christ. We do, however, offer our own spiritual gain by sharing our attributes with others. The action of it far surpasses the way of our own integrity for man is not all-adhesive. He can only share what he has learned. God supports the one who knows in His character there resides the goal of faith and true honor. I know mankind is not all-encompassed for he has no knowledge of the future other than what the Scriptures record. Follow the path of the lead in where all have the written Word to learn from. Know the work of your heart is for many to find prosperity. In this manner hope will climb forward and fruit will be abundant. I have the unity of God to my heart. In the making of His counsel comes the gain of unity. To the Israelite this means to have the faith of the former leaders who followed Abraham. He was the father to the people in where belief was given, and hope was shared. Today mankind is not faith bearing. He has forgotten the One who made him. I know there are many who believe and still work for man to have the knowing care of favor but for man to see clearly, he must invite Jesus into his caretaking. To share the love of God is a measure where man knows the Father. But to leave Jesus on the back burner is not where Scripture ends. Christ is the gift man needs to learn how to obtain a way of gain for all time. Jewish means to be held in faith toward the king even though they do not understand the unity to Him.

The purpose of knowing the Risen God claimed as the Son of Man is to partake of His offered hope. Salvation is for any who have stated Jesus is the way to life eternal. Repentance needs to have happened, and forgiveness sought. It is the making of a glorious stand of faith. God has the perfect way of operating and in His character comes the commitment of favor He supports. God is not the loss to man, rather the unity of His spiritual leading. To believe in the Savior is to align with Him and to support Him with true hope. No other knows the way of faith. The love of the King is well suited to anyone who has the desire to know Him in a personal way. Scripture tells of the way to have support for all time. It takes knowing the goal making and the lead of God to have the favor of Him tied to the heart. God invites the hope and, in the stand, comes the reward. God's gift of salvation came at a price no other could pay for Jesus is the gateway to freedom. I have the knowledge God is the one who offered Himself so man could align to Him spiritually. I read the words of the Book of instruction in where all my presence is tied to Christ. He speaks to me in a personal way due to the important claim of the Holy Spirit. It is for man to decide this for himself as for me there is no other way that speaks to the heart with clear unity. The goal of man is to find the love of the One who made him live. If the faith of a mustard seed brings a mountain forward know to invite the great One of favor is to gift yourself the hope of life eternal in bliss and good standing. The reward is to blossom and thrive in where all favor is a path of committed unity. I know the King is all-encompassed. It is by His person man finds the gift of salvation. To grant the growth of insight to others is to declare the light to them with support. Not all are willing to align Scripture to the bounty it spreads. It takes the heart a committed stand to engage with the perspective God is vested into the heart of the one sharing Him as a support beam. God will act in the way of faith and guide the heart with a bountiful insight leading it to discern the way ahead. Spread the truth and know in the wake will rise the knowledge God is perfect and good. Jesus is the way to find the favor. Gift Him to others and grant the goal of faith. It will mean salvation to those with the heart to hear this knowledge.

Character is found in the value of God to mankind. He is the center of the heart. Whether one believes or chooses to deny it is still the same truth. God is forever eternal. He is not one to allow the plan of the enemy to prosper against Him. He works for the growth of man to obtain the light and to have the heart of Him within. The light of the significant growing way is found in the value of the Creator. To know the One who made you is to perform so others know Him as true. The great way to identify to the lead of Christ is to offer your intent to Him in a personal way. Shower the plan in motion and know the offering you give is vibrant. The way of the truth is found in Scripture where the value is gold to the mind. To know the will of the One who made all things good is to align the heart with the Caretaker. Know the way to gift many is to stand with character and apply it to those in need. I have seen the way God operates. In Him is the salutation of a true knowing Being of unity. He supports my heart and shares His good care so I in turn rely on Him in a Biblical way. To offer the fruit of hope I gain is to submit to the love of God and to share it in equal measure. The light of the Creator is far reaching. Even in the dark He can perform so no one is lost or in need of salvation. It is determined by the one who places his heart in the hand of Christ for unity to be had. I know there are those who believe God has no real value. They are not in the way of true knowledge. God cares for the one who is lost and who stands outside of His character. However, the faith bearing have His full support and He acts for them in such a way light is given, and support measured forth.

I know from personal experience God is all care. He has guided me when I was acting on self-reliance and lost in my own understanding. I have the bounty of knowing He cared for me while I was not operating with favor, yet He claimed me from the dire situation, and I relied on Him with true hope. No other ever invested in me where I could say I had the love rich and deeply intertwined as with Jesus. To know He created me to serve is to identify with Him in a personal way. He has the committed bond of faith I need to have. He gifts me the support necessary to offer golden insight. I claim the Word as true and in knowing what is written so others can claim it forward is to grant my heart to the many who believe God is a righteous and good King. Jesus is the way to align in a spiritual way. It is by Him that support blooms and feeds the heart. To know the way to favor others is to act as the One who made you. I have the heart of Him within and the Holy Spirit is the counselor I learn by. Reading so I have the wealth of the Great I Am is to unite with Him in faith. The all-knowing Father feeds me with unity. He does not require me to say daily He is my Creator but within is the ability to grant Him my support. I talk to Him in faith and my prayer life builds my character. I am never losing in my stand for I endure with purpose to learn and enter a bond of forever hope inducing value. We are tied and I claim Him as my own. I know He is just and in His way is the light I need to gain insight. Reading to grow is a good training, yet to have the birthright of God is to accept Jesus as the Savior to your spirit.

Christ is the way to support another in need. Share the reward of the gift you gained and find the lead of it forthright and true. I have the unity due to applying the faith and reward to my heart. I do not stand on my own merit. I look at what the Word of God says, and I enter it with support. Both the Word of the Old Testament and the New foundation of Scripture is where faith meets the plan of God to his heart. Christ is the one who placed His body as a sacrificial Lamb so all could be rewarded the Father. If you stand on the principle, there is no place of unity then you have no favor from on high. Light is fed to the one willing to give his heart the truth. It can't come to the one who firmly stands against it. To stay at a distance from the offered support is to lose value with each rejection. God's character is always the same. He supports man and in Him is the necessary reward to create the stand man is unity to His heart. He is the gateway and in Him is the forthright hope. To value the love of Jesus is to grant your spirit the bounty of a great seat to God. The Father does not relinquish the honor of the saving power of Jesus. In God is the reasoning He is all-knowing. He has shared the unity by way of saving grace, and this came at the price of death to His Son. But the hope found at Calvary came quickly. The resurrection happened in three days and man was granted the gateway to live eternally in freedom. Have the will to lean forth and obtain the faith leading to the work of Jesus being a gift of hope upon your person. God is light and wise standing. In His value system is the way to offer hope. When we gift our unity to those, we see we are swaying the doubt and causing it to scatter. God is the one who granted man the ability to relate to one another. His desire for us to communicate is a grant of insight we share one to another.

Robin (Rochel) Arne

Unity Marker Two

The Need to Prosper Comes to the One Willing to Offer Hope and a Path to Many

The one to perfect the spirit is Jesus Himself. He is the caring bridge man desires to learn by. In Him is the plan of a witness eternal. His holy way is for all who believe in Him as the one of hope. Forever He reigns and benefits the world. The all-knowing Creator He is. To love the spirit of God is to believe in His eternal witness. He is ever forthright and true. By the unity of God to people many find the gift of true hope standing on their behalf. All can achieve the acceptance of God. They need only to plan for the hope to be their recognized way of unity. In the way of the saving power of Jesus man is fed true hope. Can a determined being of no purpose build a clear path before him? No, not without the knowledge of the blueprint. It is the manner of one to learn the foundational script of knowledge. In the same way the Bible is a read of value teaching any the necessary learned value of hope. In the pages are the character stands we engage toward. No, some of the accounts do not reflect our generation yet, they teach us about the One who made mankind. We learn how to stand in the game of life. In the knowing aptitude we contribute our knowledge and others prosper as well. To work so many, have the goal of life is to commit our hearts to others so, they too, are ordained in fruit. People who have lost their way need true hope to get back to the truth of God. It takes a witness from another. God will work in the heart and at times He is the message calling one to Himself. The gift of the Spirit is holy and good. But many times, outreach is offered from the one willing to serve so another can hear the heart of God. To love so others find prosperity is to realize you are given over to the plan of salvation and you care enough to put it forth into community settings.

> *¹⁵ When they finished eating, Jesus said to Simon Peter, "Simon son of John, do you truly love me more than these?" "Yes, Lord," He said, "you know I love you." Jesus said, "Feed my lambs." ¹⁶ Again Jesus said, "Simon son of John, do you truly love me?" He answered, "Yes, Lord, you know I love you." Jesus said, "Take care of my sheep."*
> *John 21:15-16 NIV*

Jesus is the one who served mankind in a holy manner. With the intent of Him one learns to apply hope to many. Does this mean no influence of hardness will ever be forth giving? No, man is not always a lit candle. He will at times fall into the idea he knows something of value when he is giving a loss to the spirit. The person willing to stand in the wake and realize no person is the gifted Being of unity is to declare God is the one of true witness making. Leading to charge one is not how God operates. He feeds mankind with kind gestures where the hope is fed, and faith is gifted. To know the Waymaker and to align to His way of being takes the mind courage to offer a stand of insight even where it is not welcome. But to train the heart not to attack when it is being presented with a falsehood can be difficult. I know from firsthand experience this takes patience and scruples. I have the acquaintance of many, but they are not the ones who inflict the damage. It is the personal influences that sting the most. But I do not dwell on the intake of a false lead for it is of no value. True ownership means to offer forgiveness even when the injury is spitefully given. The will of God is for man to have a heart filled with holy intent. To strike out for the sake of no hope is a damaged way of operating.

Take the respect angle and witness where welcomed. If the faith is not standing no light is given. This is how you see people when Jesus is the one you focus on. Know not all who claim the Risen God as their own Waymaker are given in faith to Him. Some confess Him as Lord, yet they do not live by His standard. Voting is reflective of this knowledge. If you stand on your own value system where is the true gain coming from? If you reject the light due to your own idea of it, you are not in a committed way to Christ. I have known those who act in this manner. Will heaven welcome them upon death? I do not have the answer to this question. Only God himself knows the real intent of our hearts and minds. I have the suture of care, so I stand as a righteous one of hope. Do I make mistakes? Yes, definitely! Should I care whether others do too? We need guiding if we are to learn the truth of God's way. Examples are written in the Book of Hope. This is where we gain the knowledge of Jesus and how He stands on issues of the heart. I do not defend the lost for it is their own demise that transpires although I do try to reach them if given the opportunity. Many try to whisk away the faith as nothing but foolish meanings. They have lost the value of God and have no eternal witness in Christ. Are they going to hear the truth one day? I do not know, still I pray for them just the same.

Glory on high is given where man believes and tries to aspire to the One who made him alive and working for the greater good. God, the one of hope, is the great way of faith. In Him is the will to know where to align and how to obtain the faith of the one supporting him. I have known the One who made all things right and in this relationship I have prospered. Where is the belief if no value is given? I do not try to assure any of the hope without first knowing it for myself. This is seen as a way of insight. God's Book of knowledge is the screenplay of manner leading all to the will of His character. Know God is not the gift of divisive ways. In Him is the only way to achieve the fruit of the heart. Knowing where to obtain the light is a plan of faith all need to gift others the lead of God. He is not one to offer hope if it is not seen as valued. Some have the work of them as their idea of favor but in truth it is merely a loss of little value. For the great way to align in faith is to press into the love of God and be united to Him in the bond. There is a time to place your heart in the hand of God and that is this very second. The willing realize God is the gateway to life eternal. In Him is the face value all need to learn and prosper. Jesus is the one who gave Himself for all to know peace and good intent. In Him is the truth of Scripture. Not all have the unity of this within. They are not going to embrace the truth without accepting Him as their own, personal Waymaker.

Do all know the truth within them? The perception of God is with us all. But it is the might of the One who made you who calls and ordains the unity. Do you know how to align the spirit? No, for man does not know how to offer hope. He can share it, even though he is not the way to gain it. There are many who have offered the love of the Caretaker to those in need of Him. They did not gift the idea, rather they shared what they gained by way of storytelling. This sets the bar for others to learn and be ignited into a relationship value of God to their being. Do you ever have to play the lead of the parent and have the advice to offer so another learns the proper unity to you? Many have this gain but the wherewithal is not with man. It is God alone who ordains the heart. In His way of presenting forward the knowing ability to gain is the sight plan all need to flourish. Do men need a personal stand with the Creator? Yes, in Him is the way to gain hope and the will of Him leads the heart. Without God man simply stands in the way of no insight. He can't fend for his own way. God is the way for life eternal. To believe in the Creator is wise and true. Man delivers his own understanding until he places his knowledge on the arm of faith. God is the value man needs to learn and witness concerning a just framework. The many who claim the Savior as true are the ones who will gain in the way of favor. God puts in motion the abundant manner of fruit. He does not fail nor will He ever.

God's faith is for us to learn and have a willing heart of favor. Do the people who claimed the right path know for certain they made the right decision? All who have the committed bond of unity realize God is all-powerful. They learn how to engage with Him through reading the Book of hope and in doing so gain the invested way of favor. Trials come to all, however, to have the King as the stand you live by is a sure way of operating to be standing in the place of hope and love. Favor to the heart is given by the One who made all of mankind. I have known God due to reading His Bible. Am I ever tied to Him regardless of this investment? To know the Savior is to spend time with Him so you gain in the way of unity. This happens where faith is put into action. I know the work of God is good for the heart but reading the Word is the way to address the care and place it within your life of standing. I now operate with God in the first lead of my desires. I have the acceptance of Him to me, but I desire to obtain more knowledge of His character. The Spirit of Him is within the page material. Why is this the case? God determined this to be His value from man to Him in a personal manner. I know it seems difficult to comprehend, simply know it is the reward to the mind and unity is gained. I do not have sound judgement if I stand on my own way of thinking. I would rather have God helping me to organize my ideas than to operate with no true gain. In the counsel of the Waymaker I can witness the growing ability of nature and its beauty. God is the one I am tied to for all time. I believe I will meet my Savior when death happens or when the rapture takes place. It is a goal for me to operate with unity in the stand of the wait. The alignment of faith comes from above. To know the King and to believe in Him is sound judgement. Have you witnessed someone who does not value the Risen King? You can see the loss they hold. It is not understood by their heart nevertheless the One who knows man has the gift of salvation waiting for the rise of true hope to mend the brokenness. I have the Word of God to inspire me and to offer me the lead of Him, so I gain and lean into Scripture. I have the witness of my life performance, and I know where the fruit has been gifted. I operate with character and in the way of it I blossom. To believe in the One who created me is to unite with Him with value. I am weak and without the growth of knowing where to gain. It takes the heart the will of God to perform so others learn and obtain the faith. Leading so many can have unity is sacred to the One who knows all of mankind.

The Jew is a reward due to the way God loves him. We learn the truth of God's heart when we engage with Scriptures concerning their value. God, the all-knowing Being of inspiration, has shown us His love value to man in the reading of them. The true nature of the Lord is revealed and in Him is the truth of His good care. Our own way is different from the lead of man. We do not know where the unity resides until we embrace the light of the Savior. God is the one who determined the unity when He offered His goal of death and resurrection to gain the bounty of Him for all time. The true nature of the One who made all things good is far above that of our own understanding. God is reflective to the man who believes in Him. I have the unity of God due to reading His Book and having the faith it is good for me to do so. I value the love of God and in Him I have taken on the reward of Him. I look to God for the knowledge of where to find support. It is far more than a time of loss in that it stands with character. The knowing way to operate is written on the page of the life-giving inspiration. God is the way to thrive and learn truth. He has not forgotten the many who engaged with Him for true love. God is the support beam man deems worthy to align to. No one who walks without the love of God can offer another the truth of Scripture for they must read the light to know what is said. God the Father is the all-knowing individual who maintains the heart and shares it with good intent. I have the gift of writing and in the value of it I hold God first as my subject detail. I have no desire to write something for the sake of no gain. I value my Lord more than the dollar I could have in a witness of the flesh. I have the knowing design of true hope, and this is what I prepare with. I enjoy reading stories of good value. I shall offer what God puts before me, and I will lead with the option of knowing Him. It is the way for a good stand in unity. Many write songs for the love of hearing a painfilled idea. This is not what sets the mind on the path of good insight. I learned the unity of God is bright and holy given. Songs can have depth except if they only lead one to think about deceptive ideas where is the value to them? Many are the ones who decided to make a dollar over that of truth being given. I may never reach the masses others achieved even so the one in whom faith is provided is the goal of intent I strive to witness to. Leading is for mankind when he knows a gain and is willing to share it. I do not dream of great wealth, although I do pray for a way to aid those when the time presents. Does this mean I must offer all I know to another? I do not classroom train, but where hope is given much value is rewarded.

I train so man can have the gift I have been given. I do not perform for the way of God is for Him alone to offer faith. I share my example of hope, and I administer the love I have. Does it look the same in every detail? No, each person I meet has a different way of being so what is connected value to him will stand as separate. The One who plans the heart is my Creator. He is the way to flourish and share the hope within. It takes the heart to be willing to align to the way of Christ. If you value, the work of many know you have the sight of unity reaching forward to gift insight to others. The faith of man is not always kind or honoring. Some follow the dark path and bleed forward of no value to mankind. Why this exists is not for me to say still it stands in the court of life so know that you must be on guard to have the knowing of the great One. Christ Jesus is the way to fight the enemy. Say His name and the Devil cowers. I know man is not gifted to always understand when he is being attacked. God supports the one who stays clear of the dark intrigue found in the gutter of life. I have no reason to stand in the way of sharing the darkness for it is only a depleted faith. It will not thrive or grow in mature thinking. It cannot change or have value for it is death in the making. I offer hope as it is the better path. To evolve in character is to align with the great unity God provides. I choose this over the work of the enemy. To love the Savior is to believe He is the way to live for goodness. I know I am without hope if I step forward in a dark way. What would the world look like if all of mankind chose death over life? None would inherit the eternal gift of unity found at the cross of salvation. Jesus is the one who made it possible for all to have life in care and honor. Among the many who have chosen the path of hope has been the streamed of faith leading to the capturing of support from on high. Leadership is holy where God is at work. I have the knowledge God cares for me, and this sets me forward to gain by Him. I value the way of Christ, and I stand on His behalf.

Will I be persecuted? I do not know the answer to this. In today's market more are being carried into prison due to believing in the One who gave life to them. I am not the only individual willing to stand for the way of truth. I will, however, have the faith bestowed to me from God. I work so others can inherit the love I carry within. I value the light and the way of it. I will offer others the testament I gained and in doing this act a witness will be given.

Care is the way to offer a plan of a witness leading to the stand of preparedness. I have seen many who have united to the One of support. They followed the way and been made upright in the making. I know I have the value of God, and I carry it forth for many to gain as I have. I look to Scripture to know what is important to know and what stands as complete. Jesus is the one I believe and have faith in. I engage with unity to enlighten the individual who is willing to know God for his own understanding. In Him is the unity all need to thrive and bloom. I do not work alongside others where I am not invited although if the door opens for me to gift my knowledge, I share it freely. My work is to tell another who my Lord and Savior is. I do this with honor and faith provided from above. Fear does not stand as it has no purpose within. It takes the heart, the will to offer others guidance and incentive to gain for themselves the love of the King. I know the work I do is not all-encompassed. I am merely flesh and bone. Where the light is given, I am favored. I look where this may gain some effort of knowledge, and I know my studies make goals come to life. I am not in the city where I can offer my voice in a church of great attendance; I know I am not without unity from God. He will work through this writing and grow it how He deems it should be gifted. I have a modest plan for outreach. I have the dream of sharing my Lord and I work to achieve this idea. Do I hope for many to learn this name of me? It is not myself I want recognition to yet, my name reflects the Lord due to my working on His behalf. So, they go together as one. I do enjoy hearing how others find the promise of God due to my work ethic. It matters to man if his caregiving is birthed and growing. How do I know it means something to carry forward and work in the writing field? I have the inspiration, and the words flow in a continuous fashion. God supports me and I believe one day I shall know of the people who learned from the care of my administration.

The unity of God carries with it the gain of Him. Do the many who learned of God lose the value to Him? Not if they apply the truth of Scripture to their hearts. I believe my Father is the way to align to Christ. In Him is the hope all must live in respect for one another. We have the plan of sharing the insight yet, man often loses his way when it comes to reading the Book of sight. Why does this take form when the all-knowing Creator thrives within it? I do not comprehend the mind of all but for myself it took faith for me to see what I needed to learn. I valued the love of God but was weak in the beginning as to what I needed to gain Him from. The value of God far surpasses the mind of mankind. He is the unity I favored for many years now and I never retreat from the gain it gifts. Leading so that others learn what I gained feeds my heart and I enjoy the light of it to me. Love is a value I enjoy and in the way of faith I gain with unity to Him. Is the idea of knowing God for all of man? Yes, all may inherit the true nature of God by applying their manner to Him in faith. This takes the initiative of reading the Book from cover to cover. Both the Old and the New Testament teach the insight of God and His Son. I know from firsthand how great the Word of God is for the heart. I have experienced being smitten in faith and it rewards me with good hope. I learn from the reading there is none other who can contribute my goal better than God. He is separate but also one in favor to King Jesus. They are intertwined with the Holy Spirit and all three are solidified yet, separate in their beings. How this takes form is not for me to explain simply it is true. I can relate to all this as factual. I have the insight due to reading Scripture and gaining in the way of training from the many who teach and prepare sermons. In practice I attend the church of the people in my region. I do this out of diligence and support. I learn with character, and I plan my schedule with intent. To offer my knowledge to those in need is to aspire to retain it for myself as well. Grant the heart a way ahead and plan on attending a church of outreach. Not all churches are in the way of truth so investigate where to attend. A church of value will commit to the Word and share it with freedom. If you have the knowledge Jesus is the One of hope, you are on the track of being inspired with favor. Look at what is being taught and see for yourself whether the light is being given. I have the work of years of training and in the name of God I offer light so others can freely learn too. This is the standard a church should operate from. The goals of unification come to the heart so if you feel welcomed know the invite is a secure hope. Watch how others feed the heart of another and learn where you too can acquire the respect of many. Knowing how to proclaim the Lord as the gateway of hope is a voice of care creating love and goodness.

[4] Show me our ways, O LORD, teach me your paths; [5] guide me in your truth and teach me, for you are God my Savior, and my hope is in you all day long. Psalm 25:4-5 NIV

God's the one who made mankind. In His value system man finds the favor of the light necessary to guide and perform so others have the sight plan needed to care. In the way of faith man finds the work a reward and that of holy witnessing. I do not have the voice of hope for that is the King who holds the title; I do have the witness of His nature to share and give. I offer the plan of salvation and in doing so the ability to retain it stands firm. I have the gift of hearing the voice of my Savior and in Him I work to prosper those who have not yet turned to Him for support. I lead where God places me and, in this unity, I am given the support of Him. He knows I enjoy leading in the way of a gifted partner who has trained to gain Him for her own. I do, however, not have the training of a scholar. I am with mankind in the way of true ownership. It comes to the one willing to invest in reading the Book of hope. There are many, as I am who have the will to gain yet do not desire to go to a college to learn in that setting. I know there are good trainers who have published material, and I invest in this gain too. I learn from others and from my own investment into the work of God. He is ever faith bearing and good to me for this way of liberty. I know no other can guide me as He is able yet, to work with another is good too. Love flows to the mind where hope is built, and I have the goal of meeting others who have the sight plan to lead in faith. Teaching requires a degree if the public is to be gifted in a classroom setting nonetheless, I claim to many who the King is by way of faith in the Scripture teachings. I do not choose to offer my knowledge in the classroom. I reach forward in a missionary stand known as homeschooled. I believe a person gains when he offers his support to the Word of God not just the degree. I heard colleges are now making it difficult to stay connected to Scripture as man has driven God from the classroom. I know I am being given truth in where the knowledge I receive is from pastors of right hope. They do not go against the light, rather they impart it to many. The spoken Being of truth is God above. In Him is the distance of insight from the spirit to the mind. A change happens when God stands in the wake of the goal. I do have the knowledge of a trained individual, still I know I need to continue to embrace the light on a steady basis. Learning Scripture happens with each invested practice to it.

I have the gift of study and in this way of work I am fed light. Does it happen in one sitting? It is a continuous investment. Each day I learn and have more unity to the One of hope. I enjoy it when He offers me a reward from the holy Word. Pieces of God flow to me in a personal way. I engage and support is put into action. God is perfect and good to know. He is the way to ordain so others can gain from His insight too. I have the unity of a waymaker only I have no ability without the love of God working through me. To work with others is a sight I haven't always achieved but now I realize how valuable it is to offer my talents to those in need. Do I always have something to give? No, for no man is the answer to another's needs but to share light is an easy way to operate in faith. A partner is one you can witness to without being manipulated or attacked. If you have found someone who stands with character and who applies his conduct to the Risen God, you are teamed in the way of favor. Goals come to the man who places his footsteps in the way of Christ. It can be simple to perform for others to learn. You need only to stand on behalf of a question or inquisition that speaks to the work you do for the Savior. Even the business of time can have a definite stand of leadership. You have a role to perform wherever

God has you placed. All mothers need to realize their knowledge can be carried forward to the child they gave life to. It is an important mission that needs hope instilled at a young age for the root to go in deep. Many today believe it is to be the individual themselves who are to choose Christ, however, without the guiding as a young child there is no thought pattern to claim. I, myself, learned at a young age Jesus died for me. Had it not been for the people in my church as a child I would not have gained the hope I have today. Yet, I know my Creator would have called me and I would have yielded to Him my spirit.

My unity to God is from on high. In Him is my character and I support the work of my own plan being that of His guiding. I value the way He ordains my offered team ship. I do the work to offer others the lead I claim for myself. To love to crochet is a talent and one must achieve the value to it to enjoy the prosperity from it. I have no desire currently to do this talent although the one who does has my admiration. It takes time to work for others and in the main way of it one gathers the hope of the Risen Savior. Do all who offer leads have Christ? No, many are simply of the desire to witness without understanding where it came to be. Letting others know where you acquired the knowledge is a plan of committed hope. It plans the heart into action and the reward encompasses the spirit. I know the way to make a bond is to offer your knowledge so others learn. I am not one to offer classes, however I do instruct if asked how I do something. I am not the leader all have a desire to learn from. For many the heart dreams of leading in a classroom environment. This takes courage to obtain the way of educating. It means dedication in the work of classroom instructing. I do, however, believe I can contribute the work of God by administering the value I gained. The inspired way to perform happens where the mind is willing to invest.

To apply the hope of math I do not deem my skill set. I am at a loss when it comes to numbers. I learned enough of the trade to comprehend how to do simple equations but much of what I learned in school escapes me now. I am not ready to invest in relearning this talent, so I do not apply my instruction in that way. I have the knowledge of words, and I enjoy working with this field of insight. Do I favor this over other activities? At times, but I have the gain of being an art student in where I learn by way of self-taught capabilities. I love to create and in the making of the work I learn how to offer others the lead I gained. Do I think I am above the classroom way of learning? No, not at all. I just have the love of being home and learning from online and book implementation. It takes an investment to gain from others no matter how you divest your initiative. I am not written down as a goal orientated person, though I do operate with character, and I stand in the way of application. I deem my work by what matters to me for any given time. God has prospered me when I operate on His behalf, so I build with Him in mind.

 Knowing how to invite one to your idea of gain is a way of unity provided from above. Small digestive values come to me where I learn and retain the unity of Christ. Making Scripture related artwork has performed well for me thus I am able to offer the work for viewing in where another can know the way to faith. I support other artists who have taken to heart the education of goal making. This, too, is a good learning stand. I am always striving to care for those I meet and in doing so I can gain as well. I value the weak and the weary but the upright show goodness too. Both are a way of operating so I invest where I can, and I open the pathway to being competent in teaching. No one knows all there is to learn. Even the need for man to prosper comes into play for those who have wealth in the pocket. A trained work shows the merit of it and in the witness, man is rightly given in faith.

 To know the One who made all things good is to believe in Him as the gateway for hope to be fulfilled. The way of unity is from on high. I stand in support of the craft I work in; however, it does not define my spirit. I enjoy the labor, yet it is not the unity I need to flourish. I have the gift of knowing the Creator and in Him I have value. I am supportive of the one who works for others to inherit the hope; however, they are not the one I serve. God is the support being of faith. In His manner is tied the ability to know Him in a personal way. This is what stands as righteous and good. To offer the love of God to another is to ordain to him the hope and care necessary to obtain the income for all time. God, the Father, is holy and true. His Son is the way to eternal credit in line with support. I have the vested way of operating, so others learn just as I have that to love God is sound, moral standing. Do you believe in the One who made you yet not have the courage to offer Jesus your spirit? You are not being fed unity in God. For He is the one who desires you to learn about Him in this way. The very support of Him is for all to learn from His witness. Death means no hope is found. In Jesus is the cure for death. He made us as His own so we could find faith supporting our hearts and minds. In the manner of favor, we are led in truth to Him. His standard is mighty, and we inherit His leadership due to the will of His connection to us. If you find it difficult to admit God loves you enough to have offered His life for you to gain, where is the favor of God to your person? I know I am not standing in a false way as I have Scripture recording this truth. I value the Book of knowledge as it is living and alive. God speaks to this in Scripture.

In the beginning was the Word, and the Word was with God, and the Word was God. John 1:1 NIV

My goal is to light the way for another to know the One of opportunity. In His value system I find faith a reward. I grow with care by enacting as God would to the people around me. I do not believe I can operate in a good and just way without engaging with the One who made me. He is the supportive measure I lean into. I have the hope of sharing with many not just a few but it is determined by God who I reach for His name. I write with the idea God will support me. Does He do all I hope He will? It is not for me to say for He is the Almighty and in Him is the vested way to gain. I have no information outside of God's good character. In the value of His creativeness, I have known Him to provide me with opportunities.

Do I always know where it will stand? No, I cannot determine how God will grant favor to those I hope to entertain. Read the Book of love and find the respect of God to your heart. It will set in motion the love of Him and in the making of the way you will hear Him direct your thought processes. There are many who believe the way to know God is to offer Him wealth of the pocket. This is an error in thinking. To offer God support is wise although He does not require man to sacrifice his cash without the measure of it being for Him alone. All profits are tied to Christ. It is He who gave the wealth and in Him is the stand of it. Knowing where to offer light is not a small thing. It speaks to the work of mankind and in it is the light of care. The unity provided from working in faith is a way to know the One who made the right path of hope. Share the idea of unity and be committed to the profession of suturing the right knowledge to those who need gain. You will align to God and in the work, others will have a justified way of being in a committed relationship with the High God of man. The value of Jesus far outweighs a gesture of favor from another. To know the way to gain is a sure idea from the One who made you thrive. Look to the way of the King and see Him as the gift of love all need knowing.

Where the Lord pursues man is in the right of his person. God is unity and faith is His resolute way. The light of God is far above the idea of Him. To love the One who made us is to believe He will never lose His stand of pure love. Faith is supportive of the goal of the one willing to serve others. Do you enjoy outreach where you tie the few who have come your way to the spirit of the Living Word? If this value is within your character, you have the power of the Almighty within your heart. He has shown you favor and in the study of His work you will share the Word of truth. I now reside in the unity I longed to have as Scripture is the groundwork I live by. The foundation of it is solid and true. No other has the capturing gift of light. Scripture is right and holy. We have the gift, and it is freely given. To worship the One who made you desire His counsel is to claim Him as just and true. No one is capable of leading in the same manner without tying his heart to the witness of Christ. The love of God carries the mind and in the path of the knowledge is gain in a spiritual way. I know I am one of many who profess the faith of Christ. I shared it forward not knowing where it landed but I do know God's Word does not return void. It is a gift that leaves the heart with courage and glue to the One who made it take form. I am not the one who determines who meets God. I am the way to share Him with courage. The One of hope is built in a way all can aspire to retain. His Scripture is fundamental and given to care. To unite with the Waymaker is sound judgement. Love the unity and be embraced with character. You will achieve the will of God and hope will be abundant.

> *So is my word that goes out from my mouth: It will not return to me empty but will accomplish what I desire and achieve the purpose for which I sent it. Isaiah 55:11 NIV*

I have the voice of reason within due to the light of the King I know in a personal way. The love value of Christ is far reaching. In the way of it is the flourishing bounty man desires. I have no ability to stand on my own merit, yet with God I can deliver the truth of Him to others. I need to remind myself I am not the gift just the one who shares it. It can be hard to determine who needs to hear from my voice, still I know God hears all men. He places the heart in the way of others, so hope is granted. All of mankind needs hearing the Gospel message. It is the way of God to offer it forward. He is the all-knowing light to man. I hope to proclaim God to all who come to me for this knowledge. I have the unity of knowing where to drive forward and where to step away. I do not have to push my agenda. In the way of Christ is support not that of no intent. He knows where we choose to operate and how we best affiliate the margin of Him to another. If you witness your own gain climb forth you have the manner of God within you. Though one may never know the value of the work he does God is all-seeing and He hears the heart of all. Even the one who has little to no experience can gift others the true nature of the Risen God called Jesus.

I have seen enough of this world to realize not all assume to know and believe in God. Many find Him unvalued. Why this is I do not portray as for me Jesus is the great One of favor. His death, burial, and resurrection are proof of His stand for mankind. The records are many as to the account of this. Scripture reads with clear unity, so I don't lose my tie to the One who made the heavens and the earth. God has carried my intent to the many who claim Him as good. Not due to my hand but the love of the King within those who serve Him. The gateway of faith is found in the work of God. Calvary is a place well known to many. It stands as the goal for many vacationing adventures. To witness the union of God to the people of the area is to align with Him in the nourishing hope He grants. I believe man is tied to God in the heart even when he professes there is no truth to His name. Why does this happen? God is not a secret holder where He hides His directive. His plan is for all to know Him in a personal way. The hope of Christ is spread to all.

The unity to God is for man to find with character and good intent. I value the work of sharing the Scriptures of Faith and in the making of knowing who is first for me is the love I hold for Him. I have the knowledge

God is far above that of man's knowledge. I am viewing the One who made me stand in character to Him. Do I make mistakes? Certainly! I do, however, choose to lead where I support the One who showed me the gift of His care. I value the Waymaker and in Him I have the gift of knowing how to offer another the will of His heart. I do not know all the details of it as I, too, am but a human being yet, I do realize how He ordains the spirit with unity to shield many with courage. Leading is for the person who has determined God is supporting Him with value. I do not speak to people on the airways. It is not for me, nor will I obtain the work of it in study. I am driven to write and to work in the art field. I believe this is the path God has put for me to acquire. I am not in need of entertainment as I have my own writings I create. Do I believe they are more superior than the Book of hope? No, for they are based in faith, but the Word holds the life of God within it. It stands in character to the read as it is thriving in good mentoring. I know I offer hope due to the gain I have been given. I enjoy the light of God and in Him is the fruit I have been gifted. God is perfect where I am not. But I try to act as He would have me to. I believe the effort of knowing the will of God can be shared by way of offering the goal of light God portrays. If you invest in the study of knowing the way of Him, you too will know the work of His care. You will prosper and spread the unity with adoration. Unity is for the many who believe and apply the heart in the direct stand of gain. To work for many is a sight all can achieve.

The love value of my Savior is far above my own initiative. I believe I am gaining in the way of character and in the motion of it I am trusted. I act as the guide to others who desire to hear the way of faith. To tie to the Maker is wise and good. Jesus is the one all need to relate with. It takes the spirit and the love of Him for this to happen. How can one stand in community without the purpose of sharing what he has been given? I now operate so many can have the wealth I have been gifted. It is far above any coin in its content. I do have a need to gain in the way of a shielding effect, so I grow in the Word and gain inspiration. I look to the One who set me on the center of His heart for I am well-tended to. I know the unity to the Creator is far reaching and in the true nature of Him all find a need to climb the ladder of insight. It takes the spiritual guiding time to evolve, and growth must transpire. How do you take time to share the Gospel? Is it a gain you believe in? Are you committed to spending time in Scripture? Do you place value on the New Testament as well? If you can know the saving power of God without placing the time value to Him, you are not working to know Him in a sound manner. Talent is not offered to the one who doesn't practice his skill set. It must be achieved in the action of doing the stand of knowledge. Share the lead and build with a gain so you can inherit the unity and build with it. I do not attend a building of worship for the sake of no faith. I go to gain a refreshed viewpoint of the Savior and how He has given another the love of Him through the preaching. It is for the benefit of man that the doorway of teaching takes form. If you are led to stand in the way of true light know you have the insight to offer a redemptive quality to those in need. I now have the covering of care due to my confession of God and His goal to me. Jesus is the gateway I have been gifted.

Leading is for the man who has placed value to the knowledge he has learned. If you apply your growth to another you have the offered faith of good character. To verbalize the work and share it in a way of giftedness you are preparing for another to author the training too. Do you have to offer your gifts and talents with no return? No, man is in a state where faith needs to receive a benefit, or he will fade away with no fruit to give. God hears the many who love to capture both character and love to others for the sake of giving faith forward. This is the unity portrayed by the Creator. I know the unity of God to His people is far greater than the hope of man to others. Jesus is the gateway to climb in respect toward. Offer the hope found in caring for others and have a witness of support to share with character and glory to God. God favors the one who plans so others can achieve the bounty of Him in the way of favor. I have the will to share my talents so many can find the faith I have been given. I do not stand alone in the giftedness for many can share the Bible to mankind. Your own specific knowledge can be had by applying the Word to another in the way you have been gifted to do so. I do not apply in a manner I cannot abide with. I know there is no other greater than God. Jesus, His Son, is the same as they are one in spiritual connectedness. What the Son does is on the authority of the One who lives within. They tie as one and build for man to gain in the same manner.

Will we achieve the same elevated state as God? No, for there is only one Father and one Jesus. The offered bond is for man to attend to the will of God so he can know Him in a personal relationship. This is the glue of growth and hope. I know the Word well enough to tie it to the Creator in a personal way. I am invited to know Him more in-depth every time I open and let His Book speak to me. It is a goal for my heart to learn more each time I have Him before me. Each page of the Word is awe inspired. I am thankful for the simplistic way to know Jesus. I don't have to sacrifice myself in any form. I gain in a good way during the process of care I send His direction. God is my gateway to live with unity. Without Him there would be no invitation to witness. Through the bond I have with the Leader of the world I am tied for all time. It is a secure knowledge I have united to. I know the Word and I gain with its term of reading. Do I have the intent of leading so others know the Scriptures beyond that of my own instruction? I do not have the knowledge as to who will apply what I share and grow it forward. I do hope for this to happen as it would mean gain has been given.

Scripture is true and good with character and a just presentation. You do not lose anything if you invest in the way and glory of it. I have the knowing way of sharing the Bible and it holds me squarely with character. I know I can offer others the light and in doing this activity I learn too. I evolve with support, and I gain in standing. The heart embraces the love of the Creator and in the making of the way I am fed unity. With the benefit of knowing the Living Word is vital to man comes the realization I am ever learning how to have faith and gain. It takes the application of knowing where to apply the heart when an obstruction happens, and pain is felt. Or if joy comes to the heart one needs to balance the offered fruit to its mainframe. I have the unity of understanding man can claim his own way, but it's better to work with the light as the guide for the heart to learn and achieve a reflective bounty to Christ. Knowing where to turn when feelings are on fire is a stand of insight man needs to learn to prosper. I know man can fail quickly without the resource of a secure intent. When Scripture is the motivation truth comes forth with support. In the making of the Book of light man found the Scriptures to be the path of hope and it was carried forth to all willing to invite it within them. I have not the work of a golf expert. I do not play the game as I have no skill to, nor do I desire to play. There are many who achieve great ability in the path of it but then what is the dream of it if it is for self? You can play and work and still grant others the knowledge you learned. In actions of good harmony man spreads the light and conversations can reflect the hope you have. You don't have to repeat word for word what the Bible holds however witnessing can bring to the heart the work of God to his person. An invitation takes root where man dreams forth, so others hear his spiritual knowledge by standing with unity to Christ. The formula is not set in stone as there are many ideas and ways to share our hearts and minds with another. The goal needs to be light bearing with character as its directive. Unity will abide, and fruit will come into play.

The care of the One who made all the gifted unity is far above what man can perform. The light of God is better than all the intent of one being of inspiration. For man is not capable of being gifted to perform so another can gain the wealth until he claims the love of the One who made him. The power of God is within man when he professes to invite Him into his heart. It takes the work of God for the unity to be created. Man hears the spirit call him forward into a partnership and that is where the growth happens. But if the will of the individual is against the God of man no unity is intertwined. Man has the capability to reject the insight if he so chooses. Why this is relates to the freedom man must decide his own fate. The love of the Creator is with the true love of Him toward all. I know the reception of man to God is withstanding in that it never breaks from the girth of Christ if it is valued and honored. I have the work of God before me, and I value it as my opportunity to invite many to work with the same gifted idea. Sharing God is my goal, and I honor Him in the stand of it. Share the insight and feast on the perfect way Christ operates with clear idea making. In Him is the stand of guiding that places the value of God to others. I know the work I do has meaning even though I do not see where it all falls in line or who claims it as a way for them to lead. I believe God ordains man to have the gift of Him in that He shares the love value of Him in a free manor. The unity and the instruction of Christ is far reaching. He never loses to anyone who determined He is the path they long to follow. I know the work of my heart is for many due to the love I hold for each person.

I plan to offer what I learn and to continue to do so for the love of sharing not the gold it may bring. Will I now know the ultimate gift is sharing God? It is if you have placed faith into action although the relationship to Christ is the best stand a person can claim. This is the measure man needs to invest in another before he can operate with true unity. I do enjoy outreach but my time in the Word is valued above it. I have the witness due to the true nature of the One who made me glued to Him personally. I look where I can apply my mind, and I favor the lead of salvation to that of any offered plan. I desire for all of mankind to have the sight I know. But I do not have the dream of being the only one to administer to others for it is the role of any believer to share the truth of Christ. I thank the Waymaker I was allowed to choose Him as my saving grace for He is the reason I am with Him in trust. He never lost me when I strayed, nor did he forget me when I stood outside of Him. It took my actions to gain my directive to Him, but it was Him who made me cleansed and pure with the washing of His blood over my sins. I am thankful for the redemptive quality of His character. I stand with Him as my advisor leading me with support. I will not offer faith if I invite a false idea to my heart for, they cannot operate together in an organized way. You will achieve more by standing with hope than by thinking you can climb forward in the way of no bounty. The truth of hope is vested in the unity to a goal of favor from God. He is the better method to pursue.

I now possess the love of the Most High. He is character and good to my person. I value Him above all there is to recognize. In Him I am made clean. He is ever before me with a pure love and goal of harmony. We intertwine with faith, and I am fed support. Do I ever feel alone? At times this can be the state I find myself in although that is the time to engage with the hope of the Bible for it changes the spiritual idea. With commitment of favor, I am put forward to offer the goal I have gained. Is this the only plan for my life? I do not have the answer to what the future holds as for now this is my idea of love and unity. I am not one to align to a false faith for it is of no value. How do I know operating in the way of knowledge of Scripture is right? It comes by way of faith and unity. There is no other option for the gift of salvation is precious and good.

If you have found the way of care, you realize how valued Jesus is to you. It is the unity supportive of knowing the character of the Savior that shines when you apply the work of Him to your mind. Scripture puts your heart on the right stand of insight gaining in the way of knowing who the Highest is and how to have Him as your own. I have the gift of learning, so

I have been given Him as my Lord. Did I always achieve the reading I do today? No, yet I knew Him by way of instruction as a person of hope since childhood. The real unity came when I stood in the way of reading truth to Him as my caregiver and supportive partner. I love the unity, and it maintains me in a personal way. I don't walk in the negative for I have Christ as my lead, and He is bright and good to all. Are there times I lose my own insight? Yes, but it is due to human weakness that this takes form. God does not lead me to fail in the way of spiritual binding for He is only goodness and mercy. I have the sin nature all of mankind does so I know I can fail just as anyone can. If you have the idea, you will never need to gain due to having much wealth you are in the trap of money. No one dies with his riches. The only thing that travels to the heavenlies is the way you performed with those in your area of outreach. If you worked to lead and care for those in the way of hope you benefited your own way ahead. Stay in the connection of God to your heart and you will align to Him spiritually. You won't have the gift of hope without this unity.

May integrity and uprightness protect me, because my hope is in you. Psalm 25:21 NIV

Christ is the way to have hope in an abundant manner. He is the one who ordained man to need His support. I have the gift of insight due to reading the plan of good harmony known as the Word of God. In it is the fruit of the heart and one authors much favor by supporting it as his stand of life. Eternity will be filled with the many who applied their knowledge so others can hear the plan of hope. It means to offer the goal God provided and to align with the insight to learn how to offer it toward many. I have the gift due to research and application. No other is more influential than the Word of Christ. He is the key we all need to operate in a caring manner. I have the work of God before me, and I learn about Him on the pathway of insight. It is character recorded to me personally. The way I invest is with the reading and the guiding of those who have been given the authoring of sharing what they too recognize as right. It means to invite the many who come into your area of life and to stand in the wake so they can invest forward the light and good intent for themselves. The unity it offers is far above that of the word of mankind. Even my writing has no foothold without the support given from the King of all things prospering. There are the many who need to find unity to God. For they do not hold the power of His stand, yet they have the heart of Him even though they may not know He is who He claims to be. The true nature of the Waymaker is to align to the man who places his commitment in the palm of His intent. The way to know the One of hope is to gift your heart to Him personally. I yearn to meet Him in the brightness of heaven though until that time I offer my work in His favoring way.

    Solid is the way to offer another the benefit of God to his own way of intent. To know the One of insight is to align to Him in faith. If you have the goal of sharing the light without acceptance, He is the greatest one of all, you miss the point of unity. He is far above what man realizes. Even where the many learn to offer hope comes the doorway of their need for God. No one can stand in the manner of Him without the work of Him within his character. Many claim the Savior with no real commitment to Him. How do we learn if not from the Book of faith? Is the value of Christ more intensified with the work of our hands or the implementation of the Word of His knowledge? Man will stand on his own merit and not lean forth into the light if he chooses to gain by the world's offering of knowledge. I have the will of God to invite Him into my heart and to lead me with His Word of instruction. There are many who feel they can have it both ways. Joined to the will of God but living in the way of no knowledge of Him. If you prefer man over the gift of knowledge found in the Word, you are not truly leaning on God for the favor of His being. I have the heart of Christ due to embracing His counsel and seeking His way of expression. Are all my choices God given? No, regrettably I made errors in judgment and lost value witnessing to others due to it. Yet, God forgives the man who repents and seeks Him and His light, so I have the way of Him just the same. I am here due to the love and character of the One who made me His own. The unity is far more than I deserve, and I am with hope due to His support. If I lose my connection to His person, I bend a knee and read His hope filled Word. In doing this I again align to Him personally and grow in a spiritual way. Faith is the work of my heart into the way of God's person. I have the knowledge due to experience in Scripture and while reading the Book I am filled with inspiration. The way I favored my Lord is to be a stand of unity for I value Him above all else. It has taken an investment to offer my heart to Him and care was a necessary calling. The value of God is for many to serve with unity to Him. Do you enjoy the love of another? In the way of it, God supports you. I lead where I am given the opportunity. With the work is the option to stop or to continue. There are times where I enjoy my labor then also there will be moments of desiring to end the outreach. The work of your heart will override the weak moments, and you will continue to believe in the way of God to many means to align to Him with character. Some view labor as hard or without the support needed to continue. There may be no influence of sharing the idea and no fruit may be heard. This stands as an offered faith not one of sight.

I have been given the labor of viewing, so others find favor without seeing where the mission unfolded. This can be difficult to pursue if the recognition never seems to carry forth in the gain. But I believe this is when God moves in the quiet so our intent shines with clear support not that of just influence in the way of recognition to the mind. People who seek to have the merit of faith without the face time of inspired work means to grant forward the love of God without the benefit of sharing in the way of recognition alone. I value the worker who places his heart in a forward motion even if it doesn't directly affect my own stand. Many have the gift of instruction yet aren't willing to offer it to those in need. Do they too have the gift of an author for many? I do not know how God uses each individual so I cannot say but I offer my own intent so others can learn. I do this to give hope to those who are in need in some form or another. I can't see all the angles of the way God operates. In Him is the unity I relish and believe in. I am not the way but to offer the understanding to it is, for me, the value of God to my intent. I hear of the character of the Living God, and I highlight the way of Him so many can gain just as I have. Each person needs others to share their commitment, so unity is underlined. God, the way of hope, is all care and no negative influence. In His value system comes the true work of a great idea and unity. I stand with the goal of faith to many as this is what leads man to a better way. Support is favor and true hope is a plan and a gain in faith. Man is not the unity needed to thrive. It is from God alone that this happens.

Glory to the One of guiding is how I operate. In the value of Him I realize I am committed to faith. I love being given the hope I need to strive forth so

I can build with character. Belief is for the one who stands in support of the Risen Waymaker. I have the unity to tell of His gain to my heart and the witness I share builds for many. I claim the saving power as that of faith not me acting on my own intent.

God is the way to live for unity. In Him is the witness I intend to provide. The spoken Word of the Bible is the hope I must operate with unity to the Most High. Glory is for Him who made all things right and true. I have no ability to produce a life stream in any form but with the favor from God I can build in many forms. Am I the creator? Not concerning the spiritual side of the gift. God is the operative in where man finds the will to go forward and produce so others find him prospering. I have seen many people act as though they were the ones who made heaven and earth. It is a weak way to believe for God alone is the Great I Am. He works through mankind and grants him the operating knowledge of where to plan and how to make and create. I value the love of God and in Him I am fed support. Do I blend forth as He would? I try to stream the will of Him through my heart, so I make things of glory to His person. Building takes on many forms. Even the carpenter of a home has the gift of creativity. It may not be that of a solid unity though if he doesn't profess the Lord is the one who made the work viable. I now say I am weak without the love and care of God. I know He is the way to find prosperity. It is by Him I work to improve my own crafting. I have the idea to maintain a property where others can learn who the One of hope is. Will this transpire? I do not know the answer, still I will offer my talents as though at some point the door may open and I will know where the love of the Father has placed me. I operate where able currently. I am given to writing in the way of knowing the Word. Will I become an author of expertise? I stand knowing God has cared for me in the writing I do and in the way of it I am delivering the faith to those who hope to learn what I witnessed.

God, the one of hope, is for all to know in a personal way. Why do we need this relationship with Him. It is for the uplifted manner of Him we find support. God is the one who determined how He would operate in our hearts and minds. He fed us His person and in the way of it we flourish. To learn from Him how to operate is to care for and unify with Him character. Our love of Him flows forward where no other can support it. How do we entertain this expression of faith? We stand in prayer, and we align to it in faith. I have many dreams and goals as all do. How do I commit to them without the value of how to manage each gift if I never have the notion to try? In the way of working so light transpires one must place value on his drawing. Belief plays a vital part in the goal itself. If you never pursue faith no action will take form. Without the stand of work no effort will maintain the knowing hand of insight. I witnessed my own failures due to no effort put into their hope. I learned I may never offer another the goal of reading Scripture, still I tell the knowledge of it to all who invest in our unity. I have the reading to know this is true, so I plan for others to gain this to their hearts. I have the will to work as a writer who places the love of God before the pen. Why do I write when I could share in other ways? I work where the gifts of the spirit benefit me. I enjoy the written word and in the making of the book material I too gain in faith. It takes time to compound a reading of any stamina. The labor benefits me in the mind and the spirit so I am fed with courage to press forth in belief. Do I know who has multiplied this favor? No, there is no knowledge to me who has written and recorded my knowledge in other ways. I still work as though others will learn and obtain a witness I shared. Are my goals just for witness making? I too hope to achieve a plan in where I have a retirement profession. Man needs to have a commission for his labor. If no gain is recorded there is little incentive to work for the outreach. God is the one who made us build for the way of hope. I am no different in that I operate with unity in the way of support. It requires monetary efforts to produce the work I labor with. In the way of it I must gain or there is no ability to continue. God knows the work matters, however, it is Him who determines if it should be a stand for a long investment or simply that of a short-term witness.

God is the way to have support far above what man is capable of rewarding. The favor of God comes to the one who believes and applies his heart and mind to the character contained in Scripture. How do we know for certain God is given to share Himself? We look at what the work of Him entails. The fruit of God is for the all-powering thought process to be one of intent leading to a formula of gain. In the will of God is the unity to see His Character and His gift of faith. It requires the heart a hope in the way of faith to Him who made him. I witnessed the will of God perform for me, so I stand as one of many who know Him. I evaluate where my ideas provide character and where they formulate to prosper. If a dark intent is present, I know it is not of value I plan to work toward. The faith I own is for my own merriment. God has not forsaken me in any way. Even when I fail it is due to my own loss not that of Christ's. The goal I must share and incorporate the love of the Creator is a witness I believe in. I gain by way of support, and I recognize the love of the Savior is tied to me in a personal way. I do not stand outside of the faith I have been given. The work of the One who made me is a guarantee He is divine, and I am not. I know the Word enough to unite to the way of it toward the love of the Father. Am I tied to the Jewish way of thinking? I have the Old Testament to know God loves the family of faith enough to offer His Son in faith to it. I do not know why the faith is difficult for some to acquire but I have always believed in the love of Jesus given to us for the better of our own way. It is more than a fleeting idea for it has stood the test of the written belief represented in the light bearing favor of the Word. The Scriptures of hope are for all who choose to gain a hand of support. God is not one to discriminate. He loves all people. There are those who support Him for the benefit of having life eternal. Yet, they are not willing to say He is the one who ordained their very being to live. I have never doubted my own unity to God, but I administer to the relationship more now than ever before. I offer what I learn so no other can claim I didn't share the light I gained. If you believe in the most powerful Being that exists, you are on the way to a knowledge God is unification to mankind. The leadership of Him is glory to His care of you.

God is a miracle to mankind. In Him we are given the formula to obtain the way of Him. It is a spiritual leading that happens and in it is the faith of all to learn His way not that of another for He alone is the way to life eternal in freedom. I have the hope of leading a franchise in the way of noting to others the unity to Christ. It is a plan of knowledge I perform so others obtain hope. I know the work of my heart is standing in the manner or favor due to the way of the King working in me. To realize God is for all to know is a unity gained where support is birthed. To evolve and learn where to witness takes the insight of Scripture connected to the mind. Leading another is wise and in the value of it I am given support. The creating side of my mind is always building so hope is found. To learn how to speak happens as a child and in the same way one must operate with character to gain the information necessary to share the light forward. Many find this hard to achieve due to the limited actions of their physical being. An athlete works to learn the game and to achieve the mastery of it. I am not given to the value of sports, though many are. It does not mean it is not valued. I have known others who work in the mission field with this capability, and it draws the sports athlete to them. Many have spiritual knowledge, and they press it forth in the unity they are gifted with. All have spiritual gain. How one determines his unity to it is what matters. I learned I am not the one who tells a person they are without a knowing care for all can spread the love of God to others.

There is freedom in our way of presenting light. God has made us all with special interests and when we use them for His glory we gain a mission of insight to gift. I value the work I have been gifted with. It matters to me to offer it forward. I obtained the will of God and in the actions of preparing work I learn too. The goal comes into view with the writing, and I am given support with its measure of unity. God does not take a person forward without first leading Him to knowledge. Apply your heart in the direct path of God and find the way ahead a delight with merit. You will learn and prosper in many ways for God is a way of favor. He enlightens the heart and shows it courage so others can learn and be given prosperity just as you have been. Share the love of God to many and in the event of it know God has carried you forth as an eternal being of hope. True ownership of God means to have the faith within to put Him into other's pathways.

God supports the love of people in where hope is present and given forward. I know to offer another the light I learned is to apply my heart to that of others. I enjoy meeting with the many who come before my path. I do not intend to align to them without the work of a glorified King in my stand. I know many find the favor to be a welcoming way to operate. But there are some who have chosen the way of the enemy, and they support me with no hope. I know there are those who have not heard the way of God and they are lost due to ignorance. But the man who has been given the truth yet, stands with no recognition to God is the one who placed the value of Christ against himself. I lead with the work of God due to the manner of God to me. I believe it is right to align to the Waymaker and to act with courage, so He benefits the light I have with support. In the way of knowing who plans to align with character is for God alone to have knowledge of. But there are advantages to knowing the way of the light. The Word is the bond man needs to develop in a relational way. If you have family members within your sphere of unity, you appreciate the value and the connection. I have the goal of offering the hope I know so others also learn the way to gain. I stand with the unity to God, and I say He is the Great One of all. If you cannot determine to value the Lord, you have no eternal witness other than to be sent to the depth of a dark form where no light will ever shine. And you will have no upright unity to Christ.

There will be no favor of any kind. To want this over the gift of salvation in where heaven is not your pathway you have no hope of true knowledge. Many believe hell will be where friends reside who have the like mind as they do. This is false. There will be no comfort so no other being of inspiration will know you or be present. Why is it to be so dark with no goodness? God is the one who made the gifts of hope. When you reject Him, you choose to have no unity with Him or His value of life and good leading. I have the work of God, and I stand in the way of favor. I now embrace the King with my entity. All my spirit enjoys God. He is the one I believe claims me as His own. I do not prosper without Him. If you have the unity to know the One who made you live engage with Him, then you know Him in a personal way. It will be a gift to your heart, and you gain in the way of true love.

> *4For if God did not spare angels when they sinned. But sent them to hell, putting them into gloomy dungeons to be held for judgement. 5If he did not spare the ancient world when he brought the flood on its ungodly people. But protected Noah, a preacher of righteousness, and seven others. 6If he condemned the cities of Sodom and Gomorrah by burning them to ashes and made them an example of what is going to happen to the ungodly. 7And if he rescued Lot, a righteous man, who was distressed by the filthy lives of lawless men. 8(For that righteous man, living among them day after day, was tormented in his righteous soul by the lawless living among them day after day. If he was tormented in his righteous soul by the lawless deeds he saw and heard). 9If this is so, then the Lord knows how to rescue godly men from trials and to hold the unrighteous for the day of judgement, while*

continuing their punishment. ⁱ⁰This is especially true of those who follow the corrupt desire of the sinful nature and despise authority. 2 Peter 2:4-10 NIV

To know the One who made you shine in the way of faith is to work on His behalf for many to gain in the way of support. To lead so another has the goal focus of Christ is to ascertain Him as the way to unity in good faith. Little knowledge can bring clear hope. Read a verse of inspiration and find the favor it grants. If it feeds you with the gain of knowing where to apply your intent, you have a witness of hope. Follow the lead of the One who crafted your manner and be united to Him with a faith that expands to others. I have the heart of God as I stand on Him for my hope. He supports me in where I am fed true knowledge. Have the will to know the King and find Him as the great One of support. He will not cause you to lose your signature idea of hope for He crafts it to you for unity to be shared. The love of the Waymaker is rich and flows with pure joy. Leading is not for the man who chooses to only focus on his own favor. If you apply your intent to others growth builds and love is enhanced. Leading means to act with character so others too have the gift of insight. If you hold fast to all you inherit where is the goal of giving? I know those who are not willing to offer their knowledge and in this no fruit is granted. The lead is not heard, and no insight is shared. How do people flourish if others do not forward the work of their hearts and minds?

God, the way to thrive, is for all to gain an inherit will to learn of His character. I have the gift of studying due to training my intent to love the One who made me His own. I value our time in the way of faith and in the reading, I have the gift of sharing what I gain. I do not lean into my own manner for it is not the great way to offer insight. The value of writing is for the one who places his mind in the way of faith. I have the ordination of favor as I gain in the Scriptures. To love what God has put forward is to clarify for my heart and mind who matters above all else. I look to God for the gift of knowing where to stand. In the way of transferring the faith to the books I write is by way of faith from above. I look to the plan of Scripture to unite to God in His way of presenting knowledge. I do have the gift of unity in that words are before me in a spiritual way. At times I may say something out of character to God; it is not intentional. I am human and fallible. I maintain the basis of Christ and I know if I have a misnomer, it will be made apparent to the reader. My intent is to align Scripturally to what I plan to say and give to others. In my witness I offer the love of the Creator. He is the gateway to prosperity. The all-knowing Being of faith supports the one who places his heart in the way of faith in Christ. He is the One who offered man His will. Through the death of Jesus man earned the path to know God with hope. The resurrection meant man was able to be stain free from sins. It takes the offered prayer of salvation for this to become the manner of the person willing to obtain the goal of unity to Jesus. I have the favor of the One who made man and in the way of this I am fed viable hope. Leading is not a simplistic avenue but one of forthright unity. Jesus is the gift of faith man needs having. To say to God, I am your invested caretaker is false as no man can do anything God needs. But to value Him enough to offer your work effort is to stand with unity to His person. Shields of hope are built in where man is granted the goal of true love. I now own the value of God within me. The means was the application of faith to God and in the profession of Jesus as King and Savior I was claimed as His child bride.

    The value of God is for man to have the work of Him to stand as a guide to others. I do not have the gift of saving for God alone is the one who has this unity. But I do know it takes one to have the knowledge to know Him as his Christ to be saved into eternal grace. In a personal relationship man must connect to a person. In the same way to know the Lord one needs to read Scripture to have the knowledge of His makeup. I have the hope to express the love of Jesus yet, my writing does not compete with the truth of the Bible. I may share its contents in expression although there is not life-giving finality to it. The Bible holds God's spirit, and it reaches the heart of the reader. If you ingest the work of it, you will find you have the witness to give to another. God writes through many today, but the work of today's reading material does not have life breathed into it. I know my work is expressive and for that I have faith it will bind some to God in the way of it. But I do not expect man to have the weight of the Word within him when he reads it. I love authoring hope to those in need. I share the knowledge I have learned due to the reasoning I am an outfield representative. I have the head and heart acceptance to share the work of God and in doing this activity others can for their own manner, too, acknowledge God is the one of hope.

An example is set in the way of what I invest toward. God has made us to verbalize our own history, so others gain from it. I have a way of writing in where I witness to man as a statement God is who He claims He is. The value of God is found in the one who knows Him as the Savior of mankind. I love the relational way God desired for us to align to Him. It means I am more to Him than a simple servant. He enjoys fellowshipping with me in prayer and reading scripture. It is the best medicine on a cloudy day or even the brightest time in your sight plan. To know the Word of God and to hear it for the sake of gaining in the way of faith to Him is a birth in hope man can inherit.

God is the way to offer insight with character and thriving knowledge. In the making of unity man finds the necessary way to offer light to many. Why is this the manner God has chosen to express Himself? God enjoys man working with one another to offer hope. We entertain in many ways but to gift the hope of Jesus to the weak is the best authoring one can contribute. There is the goal of unity necessary to grant the work of God to the one who needs a gain in the way of faith. To know that the work you offer is a reward to the lost, is to gain in the way of favor of the spirit. God uses mankind as a witness to the one who is seeking to learn who He is and how He operates. I have the faith man can achieve a level of hope needed to claim the Living Christ as His own bounty. The way to grant faith is to share it in a free way. To tell your history so another learns where to gain is to is to support them with hope. The value of sharing is far reaching when one administers the way of faith. I have the commitment to learn who my Lord is and how to know Him. In Him is the way I gain and achieve. I am not the way; yet I know of it and how to illuminate it. Share the support of God and be a witness to His character. It is for the man who learns to gift it forward. In the way of sharing is the birth of knowing where to attend to the one searching for upright gain. If you steal the thunder from another who has sought from you a benefit where is the gain of the spiritual lead? Spiritual unity is a gift, not all claim for they only operate to obtain wealth for their own self. I have the knowing way to offer another the ritual of light and in the way of it I grant the work of my learning. Is there a price tag tied to it? If it is something I can offer without the money game to be had I invest. I also invest with the idea of a future return for my labor efforts mean unity too. God is the one who has given me the gift to share yet, I am not standing in the way of wealth. Will it come into play? I do not work for the money stamp alone. I know it takes time to develop a plan for a solid name. My recognition has changed over time. I am in need as all of mankind is for a Savior who washes me clean from my sinfulness. No person can claim he is without blemish. I know I am one who made mistakes yet, God is active in my person and planning a bright way ahead for me. He is the way for me to prosper. I have no ability to shower others with wealth of the pocketbook yet, I offer insight of God and He is the value none can live without. He supports me and I have the written hope tied to me with value. I create so others can gain what I have acquired. In the way of it I too am fed light. I have glue given to me and it reflects spiritual leading.

God supports you even if you have fallen and are caught in despair. Know the way to find hope is to pursue the Risen God of mankind. The hope of Him feeds the heart and time vested makes it a support beam. The manner of insight comes to the one who determines to read Scripture and place it within. I know from experience when I take the time to engage with God good thought processes unfold. I have the commitment to follow writing even though no present monetary gain has happened. Why would I invest in something I have not been gifted money from? The love of work to my heart feeds me in support. I learn as I endeavor to thrive and, in the work, I am gifted hope that one day many shall hear of my Lord. I am very committed to honoring the value of Him for He has been gracious to me and offered me life eternal in Him. There is no better outreach than to plan for more to learn what I gained. The true nature of the one I share with will witness me aid him with faith. I learned the value of God is for mankind to believe and have the honor of knowing Him in a personal way. Leading in care is not all the work of one sharing knowledge. It takes teamwork for this to happen. Not one person alone can push the knowledge to all. I am one hoping to plant seeds, so others yearn for the way of faith, however, there are many who operate in the same manner. It is light from God when this happens. Unity is far reaching and in the commitment of it hope is abundant. To learn where value resides is character to the heart.

Unity Marker Three

God Will Deliver a Way to Know His Namesake, Jesus of Nazareth

God is the way to achieve the love of character necessary to flourish with unity to Him. His call will be heard when one places value to it. Many need the love of others to feel appreciated however, where the love of God resides faith is bestowed. The fruit of knowing the King comes to the plan of hope in that it never ceases to bring with it the ability to operate with support. I have the knowing aptitude others learn from my way of thinking. But do I believe I am the way to all gifts of the heart? Far be it for me to think I am above the holy God of all mankind! I never want to give the impression I am what man needs to learn by. I stand in the wake where speech is an influence though not the source of communication. I do hold fast to the knowing way of favor and that is what I choose to portray. It is the One of all who has the committed way of standing so all can claim Him as good. In the way of a solid foundation, one needs to pour favor to the knowledge. God created me to write but then there are those who have skills far above paper and pen. Do I think I don't have value. No, I am only one of many who use this gift for mankind to learn by, but I create for a purpose of hope. Am I the way to always know where to find it? I am not the Great One of all. Only He always leads with gain. I may invert a sentence and make a mistake in typing in where something negative is written. I am weak for I am a sinner. All people sin.

We are built with the nature within except to act upon it is not a solid way to be. I offer the light so others can gain too. It is a reward to me personally knowing I shared the light of the Caregiver. To put in motion the Bible and to practice the worship of God is a solid intent all need to declare for themselves. Think of the many who would not have heard of the King had not others stood for them in prayer. This too breeds unity to God. He is ever before the heart of man. In Him we are tied to the way of hope due to it being a part of Him present to us. I hear Him speak and I work so others can learn as I have. I enjoy working to learn and to gain for the witness of Jesus to those I meet. I am not given a life of many in my daily walk. Yet, here is the focus of my mind, writing and nourishing the one who places his faith in my heart. I have the insight to share my goal making so I offer the unity due to experience. I am training in the way of writing and artwork yet, reading Scripture is my favorite thing to take part in. God is good to me when I work so others too hear from my hand. Knowledge is for all to have. It is found in many places although knowing the value of God far surpasses any of them. Look at where you believe and put in action the favor of Christ. You will learn how to manage a busy schedule, and the unity will be that of true hope. Know God is with you when you practice Him in a witness of faith.

God is the way to achieve the love of the One who made you to learn. In Him is the sight plan all need to flourish. I have the intent of sharing the Word due to the love I hold for the Father and His Son. Unity is tied to them with me in the way of it. Know there are those who claim God is with them, yet they offer no hope to another. What is this standing as? No value to the One who made mankind with Him as their lead. I know several who stand against the Savior. They believe they don't need Him to have light within. I see darkness where they present. I have the light of knowing where to align and in the way of favor I have the support of the One who made me complete. To work with no unity is to give no hope to any in need. Even a light of dark influence is not a witness for it breeds the negative in a way of no guiding. God alone is the way to learn fruit to the heart. In His character is the retention of faith for He offers all the justified way of Him. I have no intent without first deciding to act. Where faith is built, I shine with hope. Value to God is for the man who places his idea making in the palm of His hand. Leading is that of true gain. Man determines where he chooses his value system. I have the written Word to state to me how to gain.

Without the work of reading Scripture there is no value placed upon the King. He is a mere idea of the heart that hasn't gained in the way of faith. To stand with support means to believe enough to apply your spirit to Him for the way of favor from on high. God leads the willing and in Him is the unity necessary to have fruit of the heart. Seeing the support and care of Christ is unique due to the way He ordains the gift. He acts according to His own influence. I may never have a following in where many find the true nature of the work I do yet, I am complete in the gift for I act with support to it. To tally how God operates is not faith in action. It is that of goal making not sight unseen logic. The true King grants one the ability for a purpose, so I press forth in the way of expectation knowing God influences my daily life. I have the capital to stand in the way of support for a decision of invested caregiving but without the will of God it would not flourish. I must unite with Him and care for others while I stand in the wait of action from on high. Is it easy to have to tie my heart to God above my own interests? I am not made of steel so there are difficult times. I have, however, understood where God builds good things happen. I am not interested in trying to offer unity if God is not in the way of it. I am given to the work to align to Christ before that of my own goal making. Sheltered unity is far more important than just operating for the sake of trying. I know many have gifts just as I do, and they are in the middle of prosperity with them. I do not know how God always works, so I wait and let Him invest where He chooses. I learned it is safe when I operate with Him as my focal point and mission maker. To know God's will for my unity to Him is to gain in the way of vested support.

Care is not something all of mankind is able to grant. It takes the heart to desire to offer another hope and good standing. Little is achievement where no hope is provided. To love and stand with many is a manner of faith necessary to prosper mankind. In the manner of knowing where to apply the heart is the one who can thrive for many. It is unity that breaches the heart and in the love value man is given over to sincere outreach. Where the support is found withstanding is the mantle of unity providing the knowledge to man for the sake of growth. I have the unity to people, and I am committed to sharing the love of God, so others also learn where to find the gift of salvation. God is the care one supports. Even in the desire it is heard. When I give someone a goal of hearing the formula to find prosperity, I am ever thankful for the opportunity. I do lead where given the option and in doing this action people find a lead in light. To dream of the way to support is to benefit those less fortunate. I care about mankind. I gained the will to learn and in the way of it I am given unity. Do you, yourself, enjoy leading so others learn too? It is a sight of planning we need to witness by. God is the creator who made all things good and right. He does not prepare us to be as He is, but He ordains us to offer another His way of being. In the value of Him we are given the support needed to pave the fact of knowledge to those in need. I have no way of knowing who I reached for the love of the Waymaker does not proceed me to. I am not without the hope of being a light to many. In the manner of favor, I have been given the support to perform so others find the prosperity I gained. It isn't easy to stand when someone fights against the love of the Master, however it is not me he is taking offense toward. It is God whom he directly places no value to. Do the many who found the unity to God lead with a just foundation? It takes the body of faith to be the witness that speaks to man who has not accepted Jesus as his caregiver.

> [18]*"If the world hates you, keep in mind it hated me first.* [19]*If you belonged to the world, it would love you as its own. As it is, you do not belong to the world, but I have chosen you out of the world. That is why the world hates you. John 15:18-19 NIV*

I invest where the Lord thy God has placed me to go. Do I always have a plan to share? I know from Scripture the Lord guides my intent so I can offer hope to the one who comes before me. Should I invite him to learn from me? If I can guide another to the truth of the Word, I am given the gateway to offer the value of it. Does this mean I shall have many who claim me as the guiding sight? No, for the light of man is from God. I am merely the one to verbalize the truth as I read it in the Bible. I aim to align to the work of God and to gift it forward to those who have no insight. In conversation I am given the lead and with it comes the responsibility to gift it forward to those I meet. I am not the way of hope, although I know where to obtain it. Many have the work of God, sadly they do not intend to gift it to others. Where is the way of unity then? What is the gift if not to go forth and be a light to those who have not yet received it? I value the offering I was given, and I am grateful to the many who talked to me when I was young. They put to my heart the knowledge Jesus was my Savior. Was I complete in my unity to Him? I believe I invited Him into my heart when I was intent on having Him with me. This is what I stand on as recognition to His saving power. I have since that time learned I need to read the Book of hope to obtain the value of Him for all time.

I know significant reading took form when I applied my heart to Him in faith. It came with a purpose, and I was alive with insight. I now offer my daily practice to Him in the way of complete unity to learn who He is and how He works within. It is not a way where no hope is present. In truth it is far more than a stand of knowledge. It is a guide of hope leading to the work of Him for many to have the gift as I have known. Should I endeavor to be more than an author who applies by way of authoring written pages of work? I believe I am the person of integrity and hope God made me to be. I am not desiring to stage effect my goal. I know many have stood up and performed so others learn from their intent but as for me this is not what I was made to do. I am here due to the love and the guidance my Father instructed me with. Will I have a following in where many have known me as an author? I do not know the answer, yet I have faith God can build me forward just as I am. I am a guide to the many who have been thankful for my offering to God. Is it a belief or an instrument or simply a dream? Only my King knows where my work efforts carried to. I enjoy the way I operate. It is a quiet lifestyle, and I am free to come and go with no intrusion to myself. Should this change, I will stand in the way of guiding and serve with insight. It will be what is determined by my Lord. He knows best how to use my talent and trades. I value both writing and talking in the way of page material, so it offers me a way to express my inner knowledge. The goal of God is for man to have the work before him gain his personality type. I know many strive to claim the prize of monetary gold. This has not captured me as I have always made my work that of a spiritual lead. I do need to gain cash flow but if God keeps me in the way of faith that is my unity dream. I evaluate where I am making a difference and how to learn what matters is the plan I strive to complete. I will know if this is to be my objective as God will flourish the work if it is of His nature to do so. I invite my Savior to give me what He deems appropriate and in doing this unity I know I will have favor. Not all deem it worthy to spend time in a quiet setting with little interaction with the outside world. For me it is solitude and peace. How I maintain my love is to place the value of God to my workload. I work with freedom currently, and I enjoy this stand. If I am to gain a reputation of leading this may have to change. I realize this and I stand in the manner of trust. God will know where and how to organize my goals and how to make them flourish so I do not lose my way of support. God is precious to me so I will wait on His directive to be revealed.

    Growing forward is to climb up to the way of God and to align to Him with character. I know from firsthand that the light of the saving power is from the Savior and His counsel. While hearing the plan of unity I have the knowledge God is perfect and good. He offered to me His way of being and in the manner of it I gained respect for Him. I realize not all people believe God is who He claims to be. Many stay connected on the outer side of His person. They think if they work for the better of others good returns will build for their accounts. I do not offer this kind of training. It is false. We do not need to work to have the value of Christ within us. He supports us due to relational presence not that of work efforts. I share the will of God due to Him being such a worthy King. All the work I do is out of pure joy for my Savior. I realize working is a way of life. In it is the way to achieve a better unity to those you serve. I have the role of being a manager of my own varying math processes. I do not invest in the time clock. I am in the way of faith due to my God working in me with support. I believe if I apply my work to Him, I will offer the love I gained to others. I share where I am able and in the manner of support, I have the gain. To believe in the current way of livelihood is to understand one needs to work to gain an income. But if this is the only reason you have the will to operate with character you have not gained the will of the One who made you. I am not one to align to a fast dollar. I know it takes effort to gain in the way of recognized faith. This plays a role for the believer. I am sharing my knowledge in a way I enjoy. How God uses it is upon His own value system. I act in the way of belief but I, too, am fed by the spiritual unity of the written Scriptures. I learn by way of them and in the growth, I learn who my Lord is. To know Him is in character to Him. I value His support so I work as I deem; He would have me to. The work of my heart has been granted by Him and I am fed with unity in the process. I know I have value, and in this support, I believe I claim my God with hope. The effort I give is more than a manner of insight. It leads me to gain where I know it is of God and His counsel. The light of the One who determined me to thrive has mastered me to offer hope by way of His directive. No hope makes for a weak goal. To learn with the way of the spirit is for man to have the unity to a just love. Growth is for the one who stays committed to the recognized bounty God supports. I have several managed writings available where they can be used for a future time. Do I know what this will be? No, I do not have the understanding at this time, yet I do realize God is the one who made me gifted in writing them. I work due to the love of it. In the way of support, I climbed forth to witness with character. I believe I can share much unity by way of the book material I have published. I tie my mind to the way of God, and I believe he cares for me. Should I expect a rich value to my bank account? I do not stand on this investment alone. Care is important and the lead of my ideas is for this to be given. It may mean a slim value to others nevertheless the many who do find me online have the offering before them. Should no one ever tell me they now have the initiative to learn will not mean I failed. The work itself has been an enlightenment to my heart. This is where the dream has a stand of unity. I visualize the growth to be plentiful. That is hope in action. That is where my heart is tied to the Creator in faith. For the love of writing, I learn and prosper. I am gifted at doing this activity. I shall gain in the pursuit of it so why would I not enact it in a professional way? To grow despite no wealth to the pocketbook means you place the hope of God above the work. I am trained to lead in the way I operate and in the action of it I too am given the knowledge of character.

Faith is a gift, so I teach when it is offered to me to do so. I am not the author of the bright intent for that is the One who determined the opportunity. In Him is the plan of salvation. It is the sight plan all of mankind needs to have. The idea of growing a following is for the one who has been active in the ministry and who has the gift of saving power flowing to His cast of light. But it is God, the One who made mankind prosper who stands with hope. In the way of strife or misguided findings man is the one who made this stand. God never deems it valuable to offer something false. Even if you believe God has told you where to atone a faith if it is not thriving you have not been given a drive from Him. What is the best lead in Him? To see where your heart has been directed. If you stand in the idea, you can make a difference when it comes to sharing Scripture this is an action that speaks to the heart of Jesus. He will not stand in the way of it unless it is about self alone. Then you may not find it growing as you deemed it would. To look at the support of more than your own intent means you have the knowledge God is the Father of unity. If you pray for others to gain in the way of faith, you are working so many can have the gift of hope you know. I am not the way to offer hope without the support of my King. I offer to man the way of support where I feel connected to the love of God's effort through me. I know not all talent is right and true still if you are striving, so the hope is maintained you are offering to another a gift of support. The value of the One who speaks to lead you is always that of true favor. God brings man forth to offer Him first to another. If you value the role of leader but have no giftedness to manage you are not in the will of Christ. But He will lead you so doors open in where you achieve the bounty and growth will build. To work so many have the support found in the work is to have the claim of God before you. I have the insight God is all-knowing. In His value system is the gift of unity man is needing to flourish.

I am not the one to learn all there is to know concerning every detail of insight. I have not the gift of knowledge as the Savior does. In Him alone is the way of truth and knowledge but He does witness to man how to learn. I am not in the way of support if I stand against the One of hope. I have the will to learn and in doing this action I grant others what I gain. I gain in reading every opportunity I receive and in the manner of it I am fed. The gift of sharing the Bible is for the one who presses forth to learn. My intake is bright, and love abounds. I am given to learning due to the honor of Christ to my heart. I secure the favor, and I witness where knowledge enters the mind. My character is to obtain the learning in such a way I know the light is present and in good standing with me. God is the way to offer unity to mankind. If you see an opening to guide yet refuse to enter conversation, you are missing the gift of instruction. There are situations where a person needs the knowledge you own only, he is unwilling to invite the truth to his heart. This is where the light is given, however, no intent of favor is received. It is man who defiles the love God shares to him. In the way of knowing who to claim toward the beauty of God is the recognition God is the spiritual guide necessary to learn by. People with character stand with courage and they invest when another offers intellect. Even though at times man can have a difference of opinion the conversation can lead to a growth of support. If one party refuses to hear a different viewpoint there is no knowledge to be impressed. I have the experience of supporting another, nevertheless I do not press my own agenda. I may share the love of God, yet if no acceptance is seen I step on in the way of knowing I invested but no fruit was received. God, the creator of hope, has witnessed my intent and knows I act in faith not for the sake of self. Share where the open path is found and know you are a witness to the beauty of God's holy way. Should another be in need you can attribute the love of God and have an inside knowledge God is the one to define the offering. Be in unity to the way of God and faith will provide the source of insight. Love is for the one who believes and shares the hope of the Risen Gateway. I have the knowledge God can bear the brunt of a rejection, so I needn't be carrying the hurt alone. He organizes my heart and heals my mind, and I then know His great way is for me.

God is character to mankind. In His way comes the review of the spirit He gifts. The value of the love of God is far above that of man. With the weight of sharing comes the fact some do not invest with support to the unity of Christ. I have known where man has lost the goal of God out of no knowledge to have a witness to attest to. If shear hope is the mainframe and no intent of the One who made you is within you are working to commit to man your own style of witnessing. The work of God comes into play where man has the knowledge due to knowing the heart of God from the Book of love. To invest in the reading of hope is to realize the Word is a gift of unity. The hope of the people is from on high not that of self-idea making. Know God and find the favor of His knowledge. You will learn where to attribute the love and care He holds, and you will lean forth as a child of good faith. I believe God is the one who made me, and in this growth, I am given the heart of Him. The work and care from Him are all-encompassed. I have the light of the Caregiver, and I am thankful for the unity. Sharing Him is a delight and I learn by way of faith in His heart. The intent of my outreach is for man to learn what I gained. In the viewpoint of the Savior, I am given the work of sharing Him, so others learn as I have. Does this look the same for all mankind? I have a relationship with God, so I am led to gift it to others. Why wouldn't I measure it forward when it is the support all need to flourish? All the work I planned for is based on the light of the Word. It is to me a sound way to operate. I am not standing on the gift for the sake of monetary goals. I know it may not be a mission complete as we are quickly seeing the way of God's Word come into view. The rapture looks to be in the near region of now, so I believe to work with unity is faith in action. I enjoy the Biblical way of sharing the Gospel. I read with those in a nursing facility, and I place the idea of Christ before the residents. It is a task I do not look at as labor for it is spiritual guiding that is taking place. I am in the way of knowing how to compliment those in need and this is one action I can contribute to in care. Will I do it for all my days? I do not know the length of the plan although for now I continue to offer hope. I engage with the people God places within my zone of life and in the offering of the work I too am given insight. I know many find the love of God even in their sleep. God is good to enlighten man in dreams and visions. Not all have this happen however, there are those who learn as I have through them. I know some find this strange to envision. It is a spiritual leading and one must know the God of Abraham for this to happen. Not all have the same inherited giftedness. Work where God has granted you the option. You will engage where your gifts can be shared and given. It is not for all to claim the same value of giftedness so look at what your talents are and use them to reach others. In the benefit you will learn and develop the hope of God to your heart. He is never failing so belief is part of the equation. Love is the unity binder. Faith is the necessary component of inspiration so place your intent into action and let your achievements flourish in the way of support. You will then have an acclaimed way to be nourishing those who have a stand of hope in God and are complimenting the knowledge of Him forward.

God's fame is for the one who believes and is willing to share Him for the many in need of knowing who the King of the world is. By entering in the favor of God to mankind you align to Him with support. The work of God is for the man who places his knowledge forward. In the assembly of faith, one is to plan for another to grow in the way of knowledge from above. God is the unity needed to define the heart and gain rich value. The implementation of hope is found in reading the lighted Word of inspiration. To gift others with the fruit of the Word is to offer it to those who are willing to learn and obtain the favor of it. Knowing who these people are is not always a gift given from Christ. At times the way to offer hope is to share in the way of a quiet expression where no knowledge of who gained is present. To gift someone in a free manor is to believe God is the way to all-knowing achievements. I value the way of God and how He operates. I have little wealth yet; I am fed by way of unity to His person. I place the growth of my work within His grasp. Will I always have little in the way of gain? I do not know this answer, still I am sure my God will provide for me no matter what comes my way. I have the gift of study and in the time frame of work I build where stands of vibrant leading happen so others hear what I know. It has taken time to make book material relating to the light of the King. I believe I am working so many find this as a way of unity. Do I see where my growth is headed? I am always working for it to align to Christ, so I know I am in the right stand of gain. Where does God lead the man willing to learn who He is? He grants the role of Him to the heart so the mind can be granted the vision of unity. In the value of God is the perfect hope He will allow one to offer the fruit of His character. To know the One who made you is to offer the light in the way God has given you opportunity. If you are committed to learning who made you know you have the idea of His greatness within you. To work so others, find the growth of God is to perform in the way of unity leading to a path of hope. If there were to be another benefit, I can't image for the gift of God far surpasses all else. Know God for the way of Him is forthright and true. You will gain recognized favor and be committed to Him with support. This builds character and growth.

> *¹Here my cry, O God; listen to my prayer. ²From the ends of the earth I call to you, I call as my heart grows faint; lead me to the rock that is higher than I. ³For you have been my refuge, a strong tower against the foe. Psalm 61:1-3 NIV*

To evaluate the lead of the King is to claim Him as the host of greatness. Leading is for the gifted person of hope. Whether man determines God as his Waymaker or himself, a ritual of growth will occur. But the unity needed for a stand of insight will not thrive until God is recognized as the standard of faith. A man can build with no hope, but he will not have the value of it when the accomplishment is complete. He will continue to implement more growing aptitude, though no instillation of favor will come so the heart will long for something more. God is the way to find true hope and inspiration. He is the insight to man's heart. All the growth man acquires is standing in the flame of proof upon the death of the individual. To know your work is good is to claim the Lord as the Creator and the standard of your giftedness. In the manner of faith God will ordain the knowledge of Him and true unity will be achieved. The value of the One man knows as Christ is a gift of unity necessary to align to Him with support. It comes to the one who places his heart in the palm of the Savior. It may take an outlook of time before a benefit is seen just know your work will have meaning. The stand of inspiration comes in the form of support so unity can be vitalized. No offering to God that is wholesome and good will go unnoticed. God, the all-knowing Being, of unity will gain you forward and apply you in the path of those in whom he places value toward. This is every living being. Whether one places his heart in God's unity does not negate the value of him to the Father. It isn't until the death stand when God leaves a unity to the mind of the person who doesn't believe. He will step out of the way of the goal of heaven and let the man face his death sentence without Him. It is the way of God to let man determine his own fate, however, know the love of God has spoken to all. Not one person can say he didn't know God claimed him to Himself. The voice of the Creator is real and unique. In the care of God is the formula to learn and to offer all the same unity. Allow the way of God to prosper within you and be knowledgeable to others. The gateway is tight in comparison to the path of no hope. It takes courage and knowledge to claim God as your Waymaker. He never loses faith toward His people. He created man to live with Him for all time, so it is just to know Him in a personal way. Reading the Book of hope is to perfect the bond of God to your heart. It will show His personality and His makeup.

The leading of man does not mean he is all-knowing. For man is not finite just made of flesh and bone. He is not the way to follow in favor. God alone is the one to align the heart with. In Christ man finds the faith to work so others can build and dream with character. Knowing how to operate is a gift of knowledge. I have the talent of writing, and I know it is from the Word I have a commitment to saying Scripture based truth. It is the subject matter I most appreciate. Storytelling is also a gift of insight. I have the focal point of being able to discern what the subject matter should correlate to. If

I begin to process the influence of dark thought making, I know I am not on track. I readjust my thinking and erase any parts that don't speak to the way of God. Why would I be so invested? To me there is no better thing than to bring glory to my Savior. I have no desire to write something that is not of importance. A meaningful label is to offer the love of the One who made me. I enjoy a time of reflectiveness and in the way of working so others are gaining is a love I hold to.

    I am not in the manner of knowing all there is to align to for I am a mere person of hope. God alone knows all there is to recognize. I have the insight of following in faith how to evaluate the work I do. It stands as an authoring of hope due to the content. If I fail it is not due to my Savior for, He is given to unity of the heart not my own idea plan. I know I am hope filled and working so many find the faith I witnessed. In the event I do not have outreach in my future I will have given my heart to the One who led me to script for His name value. He is not the one who stands against me. The enemy of man is that individual. Satan is the one who causes man to involve himself with a loss. I do not intend to align to him for there is no fruit in doing so but he does exist. To mention the fact of his character being a unity of no hope is to declare God alone is the Great I Am. I have the work of sharing insight in the way of artwork as well. I do not draw for the fun of the experience. I do it for the purpose of having something to stand as a picture of hope stating God is the gift to me personally. It is fruit to me in a way of support. To know it was given to me from the Lord is a hope in where I know He stood on my behalf.

    Love and care are part of the makeup of the One who made you. Both run deep within Him. Can man be deceiving? Yes, without hesitation at times. God is not of this nature. In Him is the support favoring all. Unity is His makeup and strength, and enduring hope fills Him. I know firsthand He is my Gateway to life. He valued me when another forsook my heart making it difficult to desire to offer insight. But now I am feeding those in the same arena I once was. I may not have offered any insight during the harsh period nevertheless; with growth I now operate so others have the value too. I do not dwell on the loss for there is no point. I did not make the decision for it to happen but to hate in the way of it is not a value to life. Look at the heart of Jesus and stay committed to being as He is. In the trial you will have a witness leading to the character of another being given insight. It is not for man to align to a person over that of Jesus. When this happens, false ideas come into play. Lead with the bounty of the Risen Waymaker and be fed light with glory to God. Many have fallen prey to a definitive loss due to the undervalue of the Creator. In the way of knowledge comes the heart drive of standing in the hope.

To learn where to gift another the lead of a better viewpoint is to grant the heart a repour that invests with unity. I know I was not tied to the way of faith for fear ran me amuck. I had the vision I would have no value and, in understanding, came the loss of unity. Today I earn in the way of faith. Does this mean I conquered all things of fear? No, for no person, great or small, has the will to always stand with character. It takes the mind the courage of acting in the unity to God for fear to slip away. I know God is supporting me with knowledge and I have the work ethic of an entrepreneur who offers light where able. I know it has been developed over a course of study time. To bake in the welcoming way of faith is a bounty none can claim against you. I have the maintenance of a protective hold so I do not lose the way of Christ, nor will I stand in the dark. The light has been a reward, and it claimed me with unity. I do know without the practice of giving others the same gain I will have no witness of unity. The perfection of Christ is a knowledge all need to learn. I know I am with God due to the varied way of operating in where I act in accordance with Him. I enjoy the practice of sharing the light and in the way of this I am tied to the God of man with hope. Leading so others have the work of God to give is a plan in support. One may not see where his efforts have gifted others hope although to maintain growth in a secure way is the path of trust to apply toward.

The way of man is to believe himself the limit of integrity. This is a falsehood for man is not the great One of knowledge. In the mighty way of Christ man can have unity which is a stand of insight far above self. I know I have been given ideas and plans from God yet, I do not have the ability to make them happen. Do I share this to state I am gifted? Not in the manner of no other. God builds with all. It is the one who places his plan making in the power of the King who has the knowledge He can make all things great. To believe in the way of unity that makes the heart warm to the idea is to offer your intent to the Risen Maker of mankind. I do have some inherit unity, but I am not all-knowing. For only Christ is the one who can perform great feats. I maintain I have a gift for viewing things through the eye of unity. Everywhere I see I can imagine some form of hope in the way of faith. Will I have my dream come to life? I do not know the future, still I attend to the hope and feed it my desire. I look at who I can benefit, and I say the good of man is for him to obtain the favor of Jesus. To believe in the One who made the light shine within is to place the heart in the palm of His unity. I can offer the love of Christ, but I can't make it prosper for another. God operates where He is welcome. I do this as well, of course, my spiritual attempts are not as gifted as the Savior's. He alone is the Creator who made our hearts and minds. Therefore, He knows us better than we know ourselves. I believe I can witness to another, although the reward is for the individual to learn and prosper. I, on the other hand, do not intertwine with him. But when Jesus is the gateway to the mind good intent is formed. I do act with insight, though I am not the spiritual gain for only God is this greatness. I value the heart, and I intend to treat it with character. I learn by way of reading the hope and in the work of it I too engage with support. To know the way to achieve the right goal comes to the person with care on his mind and in him is the stand of insight. This happens due to the aspiring of the Word and to believe its contents. If you apply the truth to your heart and you maintain the offering as holy, you have a stand of unity necessary to gaining hope. The value of Christ is not that of no hope for God is all gain with no loss. Work so others find the life of favor and feed the heart this unity. I do not claim I am the gateway, yet I am united to Him. Never will I offer a false idea if I stay committed to the goal of sharing the light. It is far more valued than reading a book of my own writing. But I am not belittling my care. I just know it does not prove as valuable as the Book of knowledge for there is no other reading material as gifted.

    My unity is far above my own understanding. I truly believe my King is within my heart. It is a calm presence and one of beauty. I gain in the way of forgiveness and to submit to the great One of faith is to have the value of Him for all time. His character is not a simplistic goal. To look to the great One of hope is to offer Him to the person you engage with who needs a solid unity. I have the sight of knowing where to align and how to perform so others find prosperity. Leading is for the individual who places his heart in the palm of a righteous provider. I believe I am not one to lose my salvation. It is a solid tie without a price tag. If I fail at some investment and lose value for a time I am still with my Lord in the way of unity. I will not try to stand in such a way as to test this activity. For man is not the reward but God is the unity measure. I lead so that others find the path to faith. I write so many can build upon the work I have led with. I know there are many who have the same witness and for this I am grateful. I value them as my counterparts of inspiration. Many can claim to know the Savior, however, without genuine wealth of the heart there is no fruit to recognize. God said we would know them by their intentions. The unity of my dream is for God to work with my talents and make them viable to teach others who He is as the great I Am. I look to the way of Christ, and I embrace the One of creation. Genesis teaches us He planned the world and all the creatures in it. What a mighty Caretaker! To work so others can find prosperity is to align to the way of the One of hope. I am not lost in my trust to God for it is solid and forthright. I benefit with a clear unity and in the manner of it I am fed support.

> *[24] And God said, "Let the land produce living creatures according to their kinds: livestock, creatures that move along the ground, and wild animals, each according to its kind. [25] "And it was so. God made the wild animals according to their kinds, the livestock according to their kinds, and all the creatures that move along the ground according to their kinds. And God saw it was good. [26] Then God said, "Let us make man in our image, in our likeness. And let them rule over the fish of the sea and the birds of the air, over the livestock, over all the earth, and over all the creatures that move along the ground." Genesis 1:24-26*

The unity of the saving One is for man to have hope for all time. He operates with unity to any who places their love in His direction of support. Leading is the insight man finds to have himself filled with a goal for sharing the light. I have no knowledge until I apply the work of God to my heart. To evolve with character comes into play when unity is present. I know from the Book of truth man is not one to offer his knowledge unless he is secure in his own makeup. When God is the focal point man learns to offer his intent so others can learn the will of God. Many have the vested time of faring well due to study and learning in a college setting. This, too, is a stand of hope but it has no spiritual advancement unless God is the subject material. You must pray for a gift of the spiritual kind. To believe your suture to God is solid you need to have the way of Christ within. Faith is a part of the plan for knowing the way of God. It takes the invested insight of care to Him for a bond to develop. Mankind has the gift of sharing the light and in the manner of this offered goal comes the reward of gaining in respect to God. Know the more you place your care in the plan of man to God the better the heart can unite to Him. Why this is will be for God to express but He loves when we work as one body in favor of Him. Our unity with Him is unique and in the gift of sharing His character we offer the value of unity to many. I have the offered hope of sharing, so others find the unity as I have. I know it has taken me time to unite in a way that honors my Savior. It is not that I operated in an unholy way, I just didn't expand my earned unity with reading the Book of growth. I no longer am shy and now I stand in care for those who are in need. I see where my ideas can bring forth the goal of mature hope, so I unite to those I find in my area of life. I do not have hours of history in where I preached or stood on a platform for this is not the only way to give hope to one another. The lead of my intent is vested in forms of ease and unity. God knows I am not one to thrive with intent that is high stress. It is not my idea of leading. Another is more suited to the high element of enduring in such a setting. I learn and gain in the quiet where I am not the focal point of discussion. Some enjoy being up front in the viewing lane and they are gifted in this area. We all have our own way of presenting the light. It can be a gesture of a note or a letter. Even a builder of some form can say much to another who is seeking a stand of insight. Use your skill set and invest, so someone gains as you do. It is a reward to the heart to grant your knowledge with the intent of another having the faith given them. I achieved goals due to standing on the principle I can work in a designed setting where I have no influx of knowledge from a teacher who is trained by way of classroom instruction. I see the value to it; however, trial and error have been a way of self-teaching that has comforted me. I do value the reading of hope, and this is the way to find value to the King. It is the stand of knowledge I embrace the most.

 God, the one who made you, is at work delivering to you a gift of insight. It is contained in Scripture, and you are given light when you apply it to your heart. I have seen mankind fail due to lack of knowledge. It is not found in the college setting of leading. Most of the institutions of today are playing the afront of no favor from above. God is not the unity they strive to have. The work of deceptiveness is greatly intertwined in the college of today. Some are still in the way of faith, although most stepped into the den of dark holdings. I know the man who is educated has lost much of his instruction in the way of faith. God is not the simplistic value of no commitment. He is value far above any other thing. To know the One who made the heart and mind is to have His goal of favor within. If you have been instructed to step away from the Savior, you entered the loss of His spiritual leading. I know many thought they could withstand the instruction of no favor except where is the proof of this in the world today? The leading of God is for the one who places his thought process in the way of God to align to Him in character. No offered unity is a build of no foundation. I have been in the pit, and it is not where light resides. To believe the devil pursues you is to comprehend he offers no favor. The acceptance of a sacrilege is a deceptive tie negating the way of God to your person. I have the hope for man to once more be standing in the unity God provides. It takes the heart the realty of Christ before he is given in unity to Him. The offered instruction of faith is not little knowledge but that of a great true witness. The unity to the One who made all things of beauty is the witness He is ever before the mind and character is His makeup. Travel to the west and you will see the sun set. In the way of it your eyes will need a shelter of some kind to be able to withstand the glow of the sun. God is bright and good even though we do not see Him He is ever present for us to learn from. I am not the way to find true hope. It is God alone who offers this faith. Know you have a purpose to lead and to offer the insight to others who need the way of God to be heard. The love of Christ is that of a solid intent with the measure of faith being that of His commitment in favor. He does not lose the bounty of the term at hand for He is the way to thrive and find support. In Him is the gain of knowing how to offer light to all in need.

 Scripture is the reward man finds favoring to his person. To know the One of hope is to believe in Him as the great I Am. I have the work of God within me. I know Him in a personal way, and it is a gift to me. I value the way of the Minister of hope. He feeds my dream making and, in the unity, I offer others what I learn. Do you offer hope by way of your outlook? It is a belief leading to insight. The unity to Christ is far above that of no faith in the mirror of intellect. I shower mankind in the way of sharing my knowledge in written form. Do I have the sight of knowing all there is to learn? No, I never will be able to learn all there is as I am a mere human. Man believes he can achieve the sight of wealth in the heart however, without the value of God there is no fruit. The unity of the Waymaker is far above that of knowing others. God is superior and holy. In Him we find the support of great thought processes. I work to deliver to those who find me attractive to their heart. Does this look like flesh driven ideas? No, it is more than a stand of beauty of the eye. I am not the way to prosperity. I am the one who is determined to pursue the light and to spread it to those near to me. I have no recollection of when I became tied to the One of hope, for I was a child. But to view Jesus as the holy One of unity means I claim Him as my inspiration and faith stream. I love the Word of Christ. I value it as the unity binder of insight. The way to evolve with character is to witness the light and draw to it with the care of hope residing. I now am the offering of hope due to the work of God within me. I shall never be without the saving power of God for He has claimed me as His own.

Reaching those who are alone can be a message of support to their mind. To know another who cares for them is a sight plan of beauty to the spirit. I have the work of God, and I carry it in the way of sharing Scripture through writing. Is this the way for all to claim the King? No, there are many ways to offer light. A gesture from the heart is all that is needed. There may be a person unwilling to learn the light. In this situation you step out of the dark encounter and let them decide for themselves whom they will serve. Can we invest in prayer for the lost? Yes, it is honoring and good to do so. God is the gateway to life. In Him is the vested way to align with good harmony. The value of reading the Hope Encounter is wise and true. The person who places his heart in the palm of the Leader is someone with integrity. To learn who offers the unity is to achieve the offered intent and claim it as valued. God is a unity bind of instruction. I know this from personal experience. When I invest in reading the foundation of the Word my thought process goes forth and truth is gained. I have the intent of rewarding mankind with the love I gained. It is good for me to do this action. I am not the missing link of opportunity. It is God who is the system of holy working. I value the right of Him to me and I claim Him as my desire. I shall not fear where He leads me for, He is true and honoring.

History is for man to learn the way of support, so no ill-gotten path unfolds. Yet, man does not always stay connected to the gain. Over time he loses the knowledge and steps forward into a trap of Satan. How do we not see and gain from the past? Blindness is what transpires. Israel is the example of how man loses the knowledge of God if Scripture is not contained and consumed. The heart is fallible. We do not discern the light on our own merit. It takes the work of reading the faith mission of favor. The Bible is the record of knowing where to apply the heart and how to operate so we proceed with character. Man favors his own understanding. In this witness many have fallen prey to the idea they have more knowledge than the Creator. It can happen in a rapid way. A few years' time can bring with it a unity or an intake of no value. To believe in the hope of God happens when insight is present. One needs to learn what God states about character and what it means to present as one of true knowledge. Leading is a ministry. If you are in the limelight and you invent ideas that are not of the One who made the sight a true gain you are lost in your makeup. Sight is not that of self-indoctrination. Think of the many who perished due to sin in the flood. It came due to man's hope in his own unity. A false idea has no value. To entertain both ideas of self and that of God is to claim no true knowledge for if you are lukewarm you fail. God spews out of Him the man who believes he can offer faith by way of a two-edged sword. God is the focal point man needs to offer the path of light and faith. It takes the Word of God to be understood, or no true gain is had. I know many who believe they can have the world as their unity yet claim Christ as King in their lives. This is not the committed bounty of truth. You must place the light of God in the way of your thinking. If not, you lose the faith of a true bond to Him. Many today believe they can have the dream of any relationship they desire. This is false. The Bible is clear about marriage and how it is to be witnessed. The goal is for a man and a woman to align to the King who made them. In this committed union children can be birthed, and hope can thrive. A future of no implanted faith is a loss to the heart of all who believe sin is a value to gain from. Feelings can cause one to entertain the idea it is situational. This too is a negative. No offering of death can live in the light.

> [15]*I know your deeds; you are neither cold nor hot. I wish you were either one or the other!* [16]*So, because you are lukewarm-neither hot nor cold-I am about to spit you out of my mouth. Revelation 3:15-16*

True ownership in God is not for the one who says he is the all-knowing gift to mankind. The individual who favors the sight of himself is lost to the unity God provides. The character of one who declares the sight of gain is from on high is a solid unity favoring the right path of intent. The person who stands in the manner of knowing the will of God is the mighty influence of sharing Him, so others are tied in true hope. I have the health of an elder. I am not young and spry, still this does not hinder me from offering my knowledge to any who chooses to learn. I am not the way to learn if not professing the light of the Risen I Am. He is the bolstering I do for He is the committed way of faith. In His value system man finds the support of hope. It is eternal and it maintains the spirit with favor. The way to align to the bounty is to spread it forth to all in need. It is found by applying the heart in the direction of care. It is God who offers such a good return. In His value system we are gifted light with clear thinking. A mental unity is far better than a physical one. The body falls prey to time. No hope of knowing the care of another's influence is seen if recognition is only given to the one who dares to align to his own intent. Build where you are enriched. This will be in the way of faith not that of no ingenuity. If you are leading and at a standstill look for the open path of insight. It may require you to offer your idea to one who has the means to gift it forward.

To know others would join you if given the option is to believe the gateway is in the manner of faith. I have the hope of being tied to many who feel the unity to God is vital to their desire. I am not willing to compromise this option. I have the knowing way of support due to the unity of reading the Book of light. It is inspiring and true. I know the truth of the Word and I believe it is good to pursue it. No other directive clears the heart with such leading. The value is written on the page material, and I unite to the offer. I share the balance of the way and in the adornment, I am given insight. Do I know who else may invest in my dream? No, God has not shown me this knowledge. I invite others to see the goal but to invent another's idea is not the stand I choose to do. Only the light of God will I present. I am tied to Him with faith and in the way of knowing who the sight birth is and who is not leads me with true hope.

God is at work in my heart. I achieve the worth of knowing Him and in understanding, I learn real value. I do have the knowledge God is who He claims to be. How does this come into being? It is the gift of unity provided in the acceptance of Him to you. I look at where man has gone. It is a dark witness we see today. Many have fallen into the worn earth of no faith. Why am I not with them? I stand on behalf of unity to the Risen King. I evaluate what Scripture reads, and I enhance the gain with my heart. To know the way of insight is a faith outlook of pure granting. I have the devasting knowledge not all tied to me believe in what the Bible says. It wears on my spirit, however, I determined God has them in His care. What they turn to is their own idea not that of Christ. Walking in the way of favor comes to the one who places his heart in the written Word. The love of Christ is maintained where true hope is at.

If you think you are being right by following what the world has to offer you are deceived. It is not man's agenda that will live for all time, rather that of the Savior's thought processes. He alone is the way to life eternal. I see where I have been given the truth of hope. It is not my hand that claimed it; God placed it within me. I have the truth of God, and I hold it first to my person. Knowing the value of God is to achieve the way of Him for your own value system. I am not the unity man dreams of having but I do acclaim it for my own. The stand of sharing the light will administer to the mind where to find the faith of Him. I know to believe in one's own way is false, and it leads to depravity. Once the root of it takes hold it is difficult for it to leave. It takes the mind the strength of believing in the matrimony of God's character. You must place your heart in the way of favor in where God is the light you gain by. I have been viewed as harsh or ministering a lie, but I aim for the sight of God not that of kinship to another. You, too, have the option of learning the lighted path. It is ready for you in the way of unity. If you place God above your own ideas, you are tied to Him in faith. Outside of truth is death. One cannot support the world and turn from favor and expect to be in a committed bond with Christ. They aren't compatible. Show the wise way of insight and apply the heart toward the love and care of support. You will inherit the value of the One who made you.

Faith is the way to thrive and find unity to the One of all. I know from experience one must put into action one's desire for things to come to life. When the goal is Christ the need to secure the lifetime of favor is found in the value of Him to the spirit. A love of care is a solid knowing manner that tells the truth of your intent. If you have no guiding dream to share a witness so others learn you are not tied to the One who made you. How can I ascertain this? I used to think in the realm of favor for self-interests where I learned to have the aptitude to acquire more wealth. I still believed in the One of character, though my initiative was not His making. I would have cared for someone in need, except my daily practice was to secure payment not insight. The change came when I believed I needed to read Scripture on a regular basis. It was as though a great awakening happened. People are to be given hope not just a way of life for gain in the monetary stand. An offering of light breeds the knowing way of God for it is a visible unity to His character. I know I am not the only one who felt this. I am thankful I gained the instruction of sharing the Biblical terms of endearment over that of simple motions in the way of favor for the pocketbook.

I am not the reason someone has the knowledge of the Caretaker; however, I can point him to the realization of who the God of man is. To know Him in a personal way is to believe in Him with full support. I make time to read the Book of Hope. In doing this action I claim the Word as holy and alive. The reading is a bright intake where my heart is blessed, and my influence is secure. To know the Creator in an intimate manner is a sound reward. I know to guide others to the love of Him is a visionary time of planning. I operate so many can claim Him as their lead in life. To play the hand of harmony is to record the stand of hope to others so bounty is received. Knowing God is for all who desire the gift of hope and beauty. I have had the making of a material lead, and it never quenches the spirit with support. You simply dream of more money. It is not healthy, and it won't mean goodness come judgement day. I do have to operate with unity in the way of mastering the intake I need to survive. However, it is not the goal of my dream. I am no different from another. I am secure today with hopes of monetary unity, yet I do not dream of it as once before. The purpose today is for man to find the support I learned. That is the hold I have supporting me. Forward is the dream and in it is the support needed to achieve the love of the Almighty. His character is a training I have been given. I do love the many who have shown me outreach in the way of friends and family. They are my team members. I will show any who are willing to learn the upright faith where Christ is the focal point. I believe this will mean to have an abundance of unity to God for He is the crafter of light. The return value is different than gold in hand. It is belief and harmony of the heart. There is peace in this way of operating. Desire unfolds as care and love are prospering to the heart.

Many are the ones who have stood for the One of hope. In the heart of man is the recognition God is true to His character. I have the heart of Christ for I am tied to Him in support. I value His way and to lift another forward to Him is my inspiration. Leading is not something without options. You too have the talents necessary to offer hope to another. You may have the gift of study where knowledge is from your hand. I enter reading when it is aligned with my goals but there are many who enjoy learning various degrees of instruction. In this way we all tie to the great One of offered care. I lead when the heart hears the growth. I do not invest if I can't find the unity to the Great I Am. There is no offered faith without the work of God leading me in insight. I evaluate what matters to me and that is where I apply the idea of gain forward. I recognize God is the way to find faith. In His way of presenting a hope I learn and develop forth to claim a way of support. God leads so I am given the fruit of His character. I love unity, and it supports me. To have another always near to me is a gift of favor leading me with true gain. I do know many have support from family or friends. This is always good too, but the Savior is far more intelligent than that of others. Knowing the level of commitment, He made at the cross shows me He cares as no other can. I love Him with my whole being. To exemplify Him in the way of gain to another is to show my support to many. God is all-knowing. He is always in the way of knowledge with goodness to the reasoning He does. I have the way of His decision making for He is the reason I make any effort. I look at what has claimed me to Him, and I find the faith of His character true. Learning is for all who place hope to another. To share the work of your labor is to grant those who genuinely need more unity a chance to gain the gift for themselves. Do I always offer all I know? There are limits as not all is for others to have as I do. Where should the line be drawn? It is based on whether there is a need to be met that doesn't hurt one in the process. I have the unity to realize where I need to offer faith. It is not my own unity but that of sharing the Scriptures and how they relate to me. I do learn by way of administering to those who have the gift of light in their person. If no unity is on the table, I step away and wait for hope to be granted. Not all believe in the way of the King yet, they desire the wealth from His hand. The all-knowing God of man is far above the inner working details of the heart of mankind. He knows who believes and who offers the favor of Him to have influence strictly for a unification of favor not registering as right and honoring. I know mankind is a weak body of people. Only the wealth of Jesus is what operates with clear favor. The love of Christ is more than a simple dream of intimacy. It stands as the support of man in all recognized ability. Grow the love forward and seek the will of the Caretaker. In the way of His offered hope, you will gain respect. Clear understanding will bind with support and unification of the heart will bleed character of the mind.

The truth of the Word is what sets the heart toward a good manner of hope. By the way of knowing where to offer this truth one is led to share the gift. I can learn and hear from God. I do not proclaim I know all He has to share still in the event of needing direction He is sure to teach me. Truth is for man to discern but the way of it is in Scripture. Man is fed with a yearning to achieve and to blossom with character. I have the work of the One who ordained me to witness and in the manner of sharing the light I find faith. It is the witness needed to offer to many the support I know. Do others do this as well? Yes, many have the drive to gift others a hope pattern. Teach the unity of the Savior by applying the goal of Him to those in need of your care. I am not the written character or the ordained Being of unity. I am His willing author of instruction. I know I acquired the learning in the manner of faith and in the mixture of praise to the King I am given support. I do not have to act for the thought process to happen. My care is from the One I serve. He makes pathways for me to gift others His favor. I have goals and dreams as all do although my main desire is to lead so others have the faith of God within them. It is a sight all measured as good. Even the one unwilling to believe God is the real hope to man. They may reject Him yet within them is the knowledge He exists. To stand in the way of another learning who He is means to ask for death to others. If you value many who are in need teach them where to find the faith of Christ. It is relished when embraced. If a dark thought is what you encounter step away from the one offering it. It is better to leave loss behind than to believe you can change another if they aren't willing to grow. Outreach cares to those willing to believe in God. The unity found in Him is far greater than the one who maintains Him as their heart's love. True gain is the witness God is genuine and true. It will present with clear unity and goal making will build.

Faith is for the one who is learning new ideas and making clear decisions based on moral ethics of Scripture. The pairing is intertwined with good character. To love the written Counsel of faith is to place your heart and mind in the fold of the knowing leader, Jesus Christ. He is the way to know prosperity. I have the knowing way of Him for I yearn to better adhere to His person. Lead with a clear intent and all your efforts will show moral character. The love of Him will feed your heart and you will endear Him forth to your person. I believe the One who made me is the Creator of hope I bind to. I have the inherited gift of a witness standing on the journey of faith. It takes effort to learn where to ascribe the heart. I have written valued work due to the way I operate. In the way of faith, I wait for God to work with me in the process. If no bounty comes to my efforts, I know I am not within His countenance. Do I lose the gift I tried to gain? There is none if God is not the value I seek. Look to the way of the Lord and find the path of inspiration man needs to have an investment of favor. It takes the heart to be in conjunction with the Word for knowledge to be maintained. Knowing the support of the Waymaker is like estimating your heart to record the unity of a solid intent.

You can't achieve the worth of something until trials have been presented. If you act out of haste and have no pathway to offer others the reward, kneel in care and verbalize the request to the One of truth. I have the witness God leads when we apply our hearts and minds to Him. If you are standing in the need wait for God to shine His emblem of favor. In doing this action you will align to Him with the hope of a union in the way of leading. I too have had to stand in doubt and work where I have not seen. It takes the necessary drive for maintaining to happen. Not all ideas are solid. The request may not have merit, and God will show you the truth of the goal. If you value the Risen Waymaker's talent, invest in Him and stand with courage. He may deem your plan with unity and prosperity will blossom. Future plans will come into play and true love will be the way of it.

Faith is the support man ties his heart toward. Do you believe you will achieve a bright goal when you apply your labor to it? This is the unity found by way of Christ. All who believe He is the Master of their destination are tied in unity to His character. The few who have not witnessed His good way have no value to Him. Many are the ones who place their kindred makeup toward Him. I have known some who profess no love to God. They are not without the knowledge He is real. They simply choose not to learn about His saving way. God is the creator of knowing where to learn and how to operate with clear hope. I have built so I would gain an inherit stand that aligns in character to God. It is far better than building with no insight or purpose. To go forth to gamble on a gain with no true Lordship is a false presence in favor. Satan may grant wealth; however, the eternal lead is never one of insight or good standing. God is not mocked. He will attain the script of His moral righteousness and in the making of His value is the lead of ordained, good harmony.

The lead of the one who has no insight is lost to him in no fruit. Do you stand so another will inherit the faith as you have been given? I value the way of the Savior. In Him is the moral compass leading to bright hope. With the unity to Christ comes the gain of leading that meets the heart to Him. I learned the value of working so God is glorified. I am teaching so others find Him supportive as I have. Do I know who I am reaching? No, there is no accounting for this to come into view. I have hope but no true knowledge of who I reached for the Risen King. I invite the will of God within my heart. I do gain when I pray and ask for unity. How do I know He has summoned me to Him. I feel the pull to my spirit. I invest in prayer time, and I learn what He deems for me to have the offered unity due to belief and hope found in His support. The leadership of Christ is perfect and just. The commitment of His character never fails. To work with the Lord as the way ahead is to believe He will never fail at guiding you. To learn where to achieve is gained when one places his efforts to the One who made him. I have value in the way I operate. I know I have not always been on the path of holy witnessing but now I am trained to do right for the value of God is within me.

God, the focal point of my heart, is ever before me. I stand in the way of gifted knowledge, and it maintains my spirit. I do, however, place the value of Him to my heart and the intake of His way to my person. I know without a doubt I am given hope due to His Scripture content being part of my daily practice. I have the knowing work of one who places God at the forefront of his ministry. To view the work of my hands for God brings me joy and insight. I study how I am to gain by way of research, and I lean forth, so I inherit the respect of my Savior. To love the work ethic of God is to believe in His character as that of a trained hope embodied with glory. God is the one who made heaven and earth. As a way for me to build in longevity I stapled the knowledge of God to my heart. I have the gift of applying forward the hope of a ministry, so I am working for this progression to transpire. One must believe in the work he does for goals to be made into prosperous avenues. I do not have wealth yet, still I am claiming my work for God. Does this look to be a path of riches? Not if the foot material is to be outreach alone.

I value where God takes my heart. I do work for accreditation but not fame or recognition. The only impression I hope to acclaim is that of a righteous work for God. The unity to Him is what I incorporate and in the way of the sight I gain faith. This is the notary stand I claim. I enjoy working in the way of Scripture based ideas. I offer other intakes although to me to share the Gospel is the great hope of wise unity. The love of the craft is good for my heart, and I learn while working. There is no better fruit than the call of a supporter to the Risen God of insight. Love is the value I offer and, in the work, comes unity. It is a blessing I must report forward. I unite to the way of Christ. It assures me He is real and in the manner of faith I am fed insight leading to prosperity. Doing the goals of God brings into view His great idea making. I invest in the author of mankind, and He places my ideas forward for the sake of His name. Together we are tied with a bow of courage. Do all my plans have a root for Christ? As of now that is how I prepare and lead. To gain wealth with no foundation is not something I am working toward. Even though money is how the world operates I believe to respect God is far more enhancing than records of cash flow. Jesus is my plan for the future. In Him I am fed truth. There is no greater insight than to stand in the cross emblem of favor. God is the fruit to my caregiving. In Him is the plan of salvation. It ties the mind into a ribbon of internal living that lasts for all eternity.

> *For I know the plans I have for you, "declares the LORD, "plans to prosper you and not to harm you, plans to give you hope and a future. Jeremiah 29:11 NIV*

My unity to the One of hope is for all to know Him by name. The knowing way to acclaim is a gift from the One of all-knowing insight. The glue of the Crafter is a stand in where professing Him forth as the unifier is a gain in scruples. The way of achievement comes to the one looking to find support from above. God is the one to learn from and to gain intellect. I have the gift of unity to Christ. I know He works as a master of the mind where I am the one being given hope. I lead where the heart is instructed to. The way of God is for man to have unity to His person. I am not alone in my understanding. Any who have the will to gain in the way of hope have insight and true witnessing. The love of the Savior surpasses the imagination and in the unity much hope builds. I lead due to the bounty I have been gifted. There are those who believe God does not put forth a monetary grant, but this is false. King Solomon in the Word was given great wealth when he invited God to know Him. Yet, there came to him such wisdom he failed to align to the One who planned for him to flourish. It takes dedication in the way of faith for man to tie to God for the unity not the reward. God is the one who desires for man to find Him supportive but know to offer faith to Him in the face of adversity is just as important as applying the will to gain inspiration. I lead due to the love of reading how to operate. Scripture teaches me this uniform meaning of hope. I have the knowing way of God as I apply my heart to Him for unity and favor. I know all may not find this appealing; only the one willing to learn who He is and how He presents is the one who has claimed Him for their personal Lord and Master. I am not all-encompassed. I do not have the gift of providing salvation, but I share how to obtain it. I work so many can have favor through this knowledge. I teach so another can inherit the love of the One who mastered the line of defense negating the loss of hope. Jesus is the Waymaker. He is the plan all need to operate with unity. There is no better way to achieve the light of the King than to read the Word of Him. To know this as truth is a favor in and of itself. I believe I am to be given a following in reading my book material, but this is not the reason I do it. I dream of others finding the grace of God and His way of support. No one is without a time in where they have felt lost or alone. All need to envision God is the way to thrive. I have the knowing way of Him due to applying my heart toward His plan. To atone for sins, one needs to invite Christ into his heart and receive Him as Lord over his own way of being. Is this a simple thing to acquire? It is for the one who truly desires to know God. He is the gift of support we know exists. In Him we are tied to beauty. I am not the reason for my advancement to spiritual leading. It is by the faith of Christ to me that this happens. I love my King, and I entertain Him with character. I know I will not always achieve the best formula for gain, still I stand in hope I will commit to the Lord my whole presence of support. I, too, have a lean of intent. It records the love value of Christ and in the making of the unity God grants me favor. Does this relate to the whereabouts of the God I know exists? Heaven is the call to me. Until such a time I will work to achieve the good harmony of the Risen Savior. He leads me with value and for this I am ever thankful.

The unity of Christ is supportive to all who have the value of His gain within them. I have the call and in me is the stand God is who He claims to be. I truly believe He is the Creator and in Him is the light for man to know wealth of the heart. Leading is with the one who has given another his viewpoint. I look at where man has created in technology, and I can't begin to know it for my own learning. I do not desire to understand how to implement the goal. I do have my own invested hope of sharing the light of God, so this is my path. Not all are in the same plan of building. But to acclaim God as your draftsman is to subscribe to Him with support. Knowing He is the one who made you dream is to gift Him the support He leads and implements the faith. I value my saving manner. I am not the gateway; however, I know where it resides and can achieve the goal of sharing it. I, in turn, am in the way of unity to Christ. It is a support I yearn to engage in. Knowing the unity is for the one who applies is to realize God is ever faithful. He endures the witness who supports Him for personal unity. Build to aspire and plan to thrive in the process. I have the gift of study by way of reading the Book of inspiration. It is favoring to me in a sight of unity. I know firsthand God is my acclaimed support measure. To lead so others gain this too is to foreshadow the Man I meet with true hope. God is the main field of unity. In Him we are tied to goodness. I achieve due to Him. He is the way to gain in the plan of hope building. It is for all to know Him if they choose to. I step in the way of faith due to practicing the lead He has provided me with. The stand is far above the workstation I have known. The expanse of learning is not all known. We gain each time we invest in reading the Book of Hope. Why does this administrating way stay alive? It is by the power of Christ for He is the ultimate investor. He does not change nor will He. He captures the spirit and leads it forth to glory in Him. What a celebration of favor we are given!

My dedication to the One of hope is small in comparison to His gain to me. He granted me the gift of true sponsorship. I have the unity of His spiritual leadership and in Him is the value of the Most High. Our Father in heaven claimed us as His own for the price of a witness to Him. Could we simply say nothing on account of His death at Calvary? Why would we? To know the One who made you is a talent in where hope is given. The faith of the One I know is a grant in the way of favor. I have been provided for and I am not in need. I may not have great monetary standing, but I do have the ability to buy the necessities. I am not living on the street, though many have had to. I do not shortchange the great One of hope for He is able to take any who value Him to a greater height. If you pray and believe in the Mighty God of man, you have the knowing way of His character. The unity of Him is for man to have the prosperity of His knowing way. This is far greater than all the money available at Fort Knox. I do obtain the knowledge of hope by investing in the reading of the true Book of meaning. I can't detail the length of it for there are many readings within me. Today I achieve when I apply my heart to the saving power of Jesus. He works with me, so I aim for the height of His great way. Will I one day know Him as my own personal leader? I already do but soon He will arrive in the clouds, and all will bow to Him in respect. Is this something recorded? Yes, Scripture supports it! I have no knowledge as to how this will be or when it will happen nevertheless there is enough taught that it will take place. Look forward to the gain of knowing Jesus before the day of judgement and you will not be trodden down in fear. You will rejoice and be smitten with hope. In the way of sharing the love of the Father we know Jesus and He are tied in unity. To know the Savior is to understand who the Father portrays Himself as. Prayer connects us to Him. It is a gesture we apply when we choose to speak in a message of love toward His goal making. Our commitment to the Jew stands as a sign we believe God is a good provider. Today many are fighting against the King's people. This stands as a witness to the people who have turned from Biblical teachings. They are not in the work of the One who prospers Jerusalem. I have no ability to reach the land of Israel. I am hoping this book will travel to them, so they learn who granted them the right to the ground they inhabit. It was God who paved the way through Abraham. God knew the way of today would happen. All the means in the way of transportation have gifted us the offering of travel. The Middle East is now a place of tourism. I have not personally traveled to the homeland of Christ although one day I will arrive there, sharing the light of God to those gathered to meet Him. All will believe in Him when this happens but not all will bend their knee willingly. There will be those who choose outside of the faith and fail to achieve the hope of Christ. I have not the authority to say who shall be claiming God, but I am a witness to His great way. Share the unity and believe in the One of hope. You will offer the way to another, and the Gospel will be granted.

Look, he is coming with the clouds, and every eye will see him, even those who pierced him; and all the peoples of the earth will mourn because of him. So shall it be! Amen. Revelation 1:7 NIV

God's character is a gift of hope inspiring the work of those who serve Him. In the way of a gift much favor is reviewed. I have loved the way God operates and in Him I have taken to heart where to align and how to profess Him as good and holy. In the way of harmony in thinking you need not tabulate the work as unworthy if God is at the core of it. To know the King is ever forthright and true is to plan with hope He is administering to your intent the goal of many. The love of God comes by way of investing in His reading material. Know the bounty is ever good should you learn the Word and apply it to your thinking. It takes effort to be given the heart of a warrior. I trained to know the One who made all mankind. It has happened within a timing of God that I now reside in, which is the faith of Him in my heart. I believe He will align to me the unity and offer me the road to perform the right way in character to Him. I have prayers and maintenance to believe I support Him. I work in the way of faith, and I build where the goal is bright. If I see a misstep, I know I have been given the witness of God to my person to make a change. He enters my mind, and I focus on His good way. It takes a mind-set of faith to continue to build if no opportunity is present. Know the way to achieve needs the gift of support. If no option is granted trust the work to be maintaining, you for a future enlightenment. I have a trial at a standstill yet, God has shown me more courage to continue to develop other value ideas. Fruition is in God's timing. This means to believe in Him and His presence of good faith. I know I am not the one who designs men's goal making. It is the way of God to act in the manner of true love, so I learn how to evaluate His ideas. If there is a presence of light for another and if the unity is that of a solid making, I know I am on the front of something designed to mature. When this takes place is not for me to evaluate. I rest in the stream of hope with the support of knowing God is tied to me with character. I lead so my work has value. The expectation to acclaim a good stand is how I operate. It takes courage and recognition to the One of hope for bounty to come into play. I have written so others learn and gain as I have. Will I know the many who trained to do this too? Not in this generational time frame but one day God will show me how I offered another good intention. I do have the support of His love and in this knowledge, I am fed unity.

The light of Him is for man to deliver the truth of His character. I am one who ordained the spirit with support. Am I the One who made me? No, I am merely His counterpart. Someone who believes and works with purpose. I have a record of failures too. All of mankind does but faith has gifted me knowledge and in the manner of it I am forgiven. To perform in the past is not how I operate. I have the pattern of favor, and I am smitten with the Savior. He alone can manage me with true gain. In Him I am bent to the will of His intent, and I thank Him for this unity. I work to offer others this stand, and I commit to the unity He provides. The all-knowing Leader of man is tied to me personally. I have faith I will meet Him at the judgment seat. I do not fear this as I am gifted salvation and cleansed of my sins. The Judge of man is Christ the King. He alone knows the many who claimed Him for their own Savior. Leading comes by way of support. God gifts to me the will to act on His behalf. I am standing in care all the while I transact with character. I know I have the will of God due to the dream of worship toward Him. In the way of knowledge, I am given the truth of Him. I believe He never fails therefore He will work for my good. He does not draw away from me when I feel defeated. He in turn stands and declares I am precious to Him. This is why I offer my knowledge to others. In the way of forgiveness, I have the work of favor. Many are my attributes and efforts. I look at how I operate, and I get in the way of true hope. God has supported me to the brim of my heart. In this unity I gain insight with value. I lead so others hear as I have. It takes the heart the stand of gain before it can prosper. To learn is to offer the heart and mind a plan. If the knowing will of your character is to gift another you learned the unity to God is for any who claim Him as God. I, too, have sunk in the way of no light being grafted but it was there waiting for me to aspire to it. I have the work of one who is creative yet, does not administer it until the timing of God has been granted. I share where I am given the ability, and I know my order of the day is to offer hope to those in need. I have the value of God, so I gain by way of His counsel. The richness of God is for all to inherit. The love of God is for the willing to claim. If you stand at a distance, it is your own loss not that of others. Look to the brightness of the Savior and find the faith you need to flourish.

Unity Marker Four

The Land of Israel is not for Others but for the Jewish Nation Itself

The unity in the way of support is from on high. The way of God is to ordain the need and declare it a manner of His intent. How does this happen if not for the one of kinship to Christ? I have been gifted with the ability to create and, in the work, I have the idea of claiming the One of light. I make detailed artwork so others can be fed courage. Leading is the bounty of witness I esteem as good. To know the One of creation is to align to Him in character. The love of God is far reaching. Know to believe is to offer another the right of His hope and His makeup. Read Scripture to know where to present the love of Christ to many. We find people are not so different from one to another. Lead with the intent of unity. It is prospering to the honor of Christ. To know the way of a soldier is to have placed your heart within the manner of his commitment to live freely. This nation is filled with opportunity. Where one desires to learn it can be vested. Our commitment to God should be a solid goal for all time. Know the way to give another the support is to stand in the gift of His goal making. I have no idea where I will proceed to, yet I know I have the unity of God to my heart. I act in accordance with the One of light and in this committed value stands support. God never fails nor does He leave the dream of someone's love value. If you have achievements but no forthright way to present them to another wait for God to gift you the platform and the manner of insight. It can be a reward to know God is at work on your behalf. Gifting support in the wait time shows character and contributes to those who are less fortunate. God is a labor force so invite His honor to your entertained dream. You will show unity and in the making of Him to your heart you will have the faith to build and continue to prosper. It may be that of sharing your idea so another too can be part of the unity. I express my hope to those willing to learn my goals. I do not demand another to love the dream as I have. This is foolish to offer light if it is not intended for their influence. Work may be a derivative for the hard line of clear favor. Labor brings to the workforce the expectation earnings will come. I have had to offer others labor without benefiting from the value. It took time for the will of God to be revealed. The source of my dream building comes from God. I know He is the witness to me.

    I am glue to the ones who are committed to learning the value of God and His personal training is within them. I believe I am in the way of faith, and I stand with character. I hope to build so many have the offered favor I have been gifted. I am not the only one who invites the Lord to his heart. It takes the mind of the warrior to determine the unity is worth embracing. I am the lead in a crowd online. I offer a way to pray and to find support. I do this so others can embrace the knowledge I gained. I learn at the same pace, and I share the truth, so others are fed inspiration. By voicing hope many have the same incentive to offer others the moral gain just as I do. Team building happens when one individual believes he can make a difference. I am not the only one doing this activity. It resides in the plan of many. To apply the faith into action is to place your heart in the way of God to learn. I am not the sounding board I am the profit of a learned intent. Scripture has shown me I can support the man who gains by my hand. Do I have the knowledge of whom I offered the light to? No, I do not have the knowledge to this. I am writing in the way of intent. I maintain the knowing aptitude God delivers on His care. Even though I have not inherited thoughts of wealth I know God can offer me a goal by way of work ethic. The profound way of faith is for the One who gave me the courage and the ability. He asked me to operate with His support. I yearn to plan for others. It has been unity to God that has brought me to this plateau. The faith of someone who offers what he learns is shown to be a stand of support where much unity is seen. Knowing the heart of God is something on going. The more you read truth the better your unity is to Him. I have the intent of always applying my goals to His counsel. It is a matter of effort that this builds. I gifted others knowledge in the way of reading aloud so they too hear the truth. I do not have the intent of always being on the inside of no knowledge for man needs to see his progress or he loses hope. God knows my every thought. In Him is the plan of salvation and this is the way I operate. To know another is gaining due to my work is to be given the inspiration to work for God for others are valued just as I am. My covering of truth is shared in a diligent way. I practice work ethic, and I believe the reward will build. Stand with courage and know God is ever faithful. You will lead and grow with prosperity in faith.

The certainty of the way of God is found in the power of His name. Scripture is the gift of knowing who the Lord is and how He operates. The witness to Him is the many who claimed Him as Lord. The will and character of His makeup is far above that of any other. Seeing Him as a caregiver is wise and unity is present. To lead so another can gain unity is to deliver it toward a common stand. I am in the way of faith due to applying my inner thought process to His person. I invite my God to me by reading the Book of hope. I am tied to His care when I engage in this manner. Fruit is fulfilled and goal making builds. I thank my King for His witness, and I am made righteous due to Him. I am tied to His character and in the way of it I am fed light. The One who placed me to Him is Jesus the great One! I enter the witness stand and record the volume of gifted light in the bounty I am given. I share the hope, and I am given offerings back in return. Is there a limit with the One of hope? No, He does not end in His caregiving. He doesn't' run out of faith for you nor will He ever. I am inclined to agree with the One of inspiration due to the way He has shown me favor. I have goals outside of my own understanding or accomplishments. I am not a small insignificant lead. I place my dreams and hopes in the palm of His hand. He, in turn, delivers to me a gift of hope. I build in the way of intent so others can thrive and be fed too. Look to where the light of the Savior is found. It can be had with perfection. The Book of hope is the vested meal we inhale with true love. Where this stands is in the light for it is holy and true. I know the work of my heart is not simplistic. It is depth and love entangled. The pure way of faith comes to the one who places his insight into the lead of Scripture. The value of it far exceeds the mind. A gift of insight will gather in unity, and you will gain the ability to push forth a new idea or hope. I have the instruction of reading so words for me come with insight. I studied as a child and into adulthood. It meant to train and to grant my head the sight of knowing the alphabet along with grammar and spelling. Should I reverse and go back to more education? This is not how I operate. I desire to engage with truth in reading then applying it in character to my study habits. I write once I reviewed the love of the Creator. He is precious to me! I believe the stand of this makes the work more genuine to His person. I have the witness of sharing God and in the work ethic I am given unity.

> *²Be completely humble and gentle; be patient, bearing one another in love. ³Make every effort to keep the unity of the Spirit through the bond of peace. Ephesians 4:2-3 NIV*

The care of the Almighty is a reward and a benefit. He never forgets the one who believes and acts as though He is intentional. The true bond of God is mighty and holy. In Him we find the faith to build and create. I have many dreams at this present hour. Will they come to be? I do not know for I am not privy to this knowledge. But I believe God is at work with my dream making. In His way of presenting inspiration, I have been gifted with scenic ideas others have not gained. I offer hope to many and in the way of faith I stand in complete awe of the King who adorns me to Him. The value of knowing the lighted way cannot be measured. I am tied to the Savior and His goal making. I learn due to the application of reading Scripture, so my heart can hear the Word and support Christ. I know the New Testament supports the man who places his honor toward the Creator of it. I am not alone in the knowledge of faith for there are a great number who relate to this unity. I invested my desire to the great One of insight and in doing the labor I am given care. I stand with support when I fear or think I am losing my way. The admittance of Christ changes the heart and offers it a way ahead. Love is the committed way God operates. He is ever before the believer and the man who adheres to Him with support. God will work where welcome to do so. In the gift of a learned skill a magnet of truth will be witnessed. Where do you learn best? I enjoy self-application. I look at a resource and believe there is a way to achieve the pattern. I am not a draw in the art field, but I am working to be. Do I have the answer before the unity is seen? No, God is the support I learn by. At times an idea is presented, and I know God granted it to me. I invest and take time to apply. If I am stumped, I know I need to research how others have found the passage to exist. If there is no other who has done as I envision, I know I am to decipher from the God of all what my unity is to look like. He will ordain to my heart what is necessary to learn. I have the gift of His person, so I know there is an answer to discover. At times I hear the voice of the King, and I gain in this manner. God has given me care and I love Him for this unity! To perfect a dream is the commitment one needs to believe God is at work on his behalf. Many have the term limit due to no value to their own ability. I am weak at times when it comes to faith within me. Not that I doubt God, rather my own self. I must realign my unity and place my measure of hope upon the thrown of the One who made me in His own image. I value the knit way we communicate. For me it is a sound goal to have the witness of Jesus on my behalf. Character is a unity to Him and in the manner of faith it professes God to be the great way!

Character is the solid hope I maintain. I have no heart for the dark way of life. I do not offer false narratives, and I am not willing to abolish the faith in Christ for the value of a cent no matter how many of them present to me. I unify to Christ and in the measure of knowing Him I am gifted the intent of wisdom over cash value. I lead that others too can have a gift of instructed hope. It may be simple knowledge or one of enrichment leading to support. True hope is built by offering the One of faith your knowledge. It grows forth and multiplies so many have the witness of faith for their own unity. I have the identity of sharing the plan of salvation. It far exceeds my other dreams of recognition. The title of administrator is not the witness I hold to, though it is a stand of my growing ability. God supports my heart, and He showers me with it. When others have rejected my favor, I stand on behalf of who made me, and I incorporate the time at hand. Is the benefit for others a good inspiration or is this for me alone? It stands to reason if many can enjoy your plan God is value to it but there must be the reconciled lead of true witness making. If you have goals of wealth with no intent to guide another where is the hope to come from? We are to guide others to the Creator. This can be an idea in the making where others receive joy or unity by way of fellowship. A return will come so know God has the idea in the fold of His hem. I am not one to quickly judge what is being crafted. I act where I am led and if I see a path of hope I work for the favor of it. It may require me to stand for a period where no productivity takes root. In the wait God has supported me and I tied to His character through the draw. I am not the gifted One who knows all the ins and outs of the production. It may be others are bound to the plan, and they need growth. To yearn and stay standing is to believe the Father has hope enough for you for any goal achievement.

Lead in the way God has granted you favor. Not all have the same skill set so enter the arena with your own invested hope. I am not the One who made you so I can't comment on whether you will succeed. It takes the mind and the heart to be vested plus the work ethic to claim to the risen goal. I failed often due to no stand of faith in myself. Today I am more inclined to claim the power of God and to witness Him as the source of a dream not that of another. I used to wait for others to join me in my work. It bred little attendance. I learned not all have the same idea or the way of it within them. I have the knowledge God is the one who ordains the heart and builds it to hope. I am striving to gain so I administer to those where able. Open doors mean to press forward and apply in the way of unity. God is skilled so I don't have to have all the means for He can bring to me what is necessary to operate the formula. It has taken time for me to gain this hope. I was not one to learn from the classroom setting. My preference has always been hands on training. It has been a growing way for me where I gain in the audience of self. God has led me to the unity in myself. I am willing to learn from others, although this is not my preferred way. I have other gifts where I work with those who have the skill set and I know it is a necessity for me. I invite all to learn and to apply but know we all must find what works best for our own way of learning. Should I ever need to attend a level of education outside of my gifted stand I will not hesitate to advance but God knows me better, so I don't anticipate this happening. I ensure my growth by reading the Book of wealth.

Scripture opens the mind to knowledge in where a textbook of another implementation will not. How this happens is by Christ's good way. I learned this to be true for my own unity. I now accept I am limited in areas, yet this does not discourage me. God has supported me with many talents others do not have so I see a way for me to lead. In the way of it I press into those who come before me with hope. I share intellect and I witness the truth I learned. Do all agree with what I determine? No, for not all see things as I do still, I know where my faith lies. I esteem the Word of God to be light. I gain from reading the intake and I know I am saved due to the Risen King and His salvation gift. For me the best way to offer hope is to relay the truth of this to others.

Stand with integrity and learn from the Israelites who is the One to bond with. Scripture in the Old Testament is solid, however, the New Testament speaks to the light of God to His people. I am tying in the truth of God to those who believe He is all-knowing. I relate to Christ as He claimed He was torn due the whipping He withstood. The crucifixion created a way for man to have the birth to know God and who He is to him. I am one of His beings. I walk due to Him desiring for me to do so. I am not small when it comes to the favor of God to my heart. I am tied to Him as I hope to share Him with all in my region. I work with the intent of God, so I offer light. As a member of a group page, I share who God is to all. I do not discriminate. I accept outside the region if someone applies to my study. I am working so all can claim the unity I have. It is not a small thing to offer hope to others. It can mean the stand of unity is given where man finds the love of the Savior for himself. I do not learn who has offered his heart to Christ for it is not expressed to me. I invite the Word forward and let God do the claiming. I have not the will to try to learn who all has gained for this would be self-goals then. I look to God for the glory to be gifted. He is the one who never pursues a dark reward, and in His care, I am gifted unity. I thank Him for this reward. It is far more than I deserve. I am a sinner as all of mankind is. We need the Master to call us to Him. He does this when the timing is right to accomplish the unity. I was a child when this happened to me, except it took adulthood for it to be flourishing. To unite to God in favor is to read the Book of His teaching.

The Bible records God's character. This is where you learn who He is and how He operates. I am not the only investment of good counsel He is making. Any who strive to gain from the perspective God is the great, mighty love of all are the people who believe in Him with their whole support. Growth in unity happens where the truth is recorded. My heart hears the truth, and it incorporates it into my mind. In this way I think in terms of endearment in place of the negative. I know many believe they act with good favor however, the Bible states not one person shall stand on his own. You must know God to enter the gate of heaven. My belief in Him is to tie my spirit to His counsel. I operate so God is given my hope. In turn He delivers to me an abundance of good favor. He is spiritual. In His value system is gold to the being of His creation. All who claim Him as Lord are given the knowledge, He is ever faithful.

My heart is tied as the Israelite who has given his whole being to the Savior. Do people of all regions know Christ? Many have the head knowledge to Him. I have the gift of salvation due to applying faith in His direct line of unity. I embrace Him with all I have. Do I make mistakes at times? Yes, for sure! But I am just a person of hope not the Almighty. In the caregiving department I am favored. It is how I maintain my self-worth. I look to the way of God, and I learn where to offer my intelligence. I am not the only person willing to align to the Lord for He has many followers. Even the meaning to His name stands as righteousness. I value it above all others. To swear in vain is to go against the light and to portray a dark lead in the manner of no support. Swearing is a lifestyle for many. They know not what they are saying for each cussword stands against the spirit. I have value to my way of thinking, so I offer hope in the way of staying in time with character. Yes, I do slip up, though it is not with intent. It is natural to lose your words when something meaningful happens and it is difficult to stay calm. I practic the Word, so it maintains me with support. I do not enjoy a conversation where men speak false decrees including cusswords of no value. If you say false things for the fun of expression, you are lost to the unity God provides.

I am not one to condemn others. I simply do not continue to engage if no unity is witnessed. Many find this style of hope a gesture against them. It is not that; rather a need for my own character to give bright insight. I am not an all-gifted word speaker. I do not intend to portray this. I have the support of knowing false words have no value, so I do not use them in daily practice. It is a choice how one values his speaking gifts. I elect to say words of light with support, so others are fed true gain. Does it mean I have all the giftedness to never say something out of character? No, for I am made of flesh as are all of mankind. I simply try to say things of goodness not harm. I see where the light is, and I hope to be present within it. I ask for the gift of unity to my Creator and in His way, I find peace. It means to attend to my own support where His way is perfect and mine is not. Shoulder the way of

God and stand with Him so others learn from your witness. It means to align to Him with unity not self-origination.

Leading is for the man who places Christ in the center of his gain. I am not the all-knowing One of light, but I find it in the true Word of insight. Unity teaches me where to master my intellect. I have the hope to offer this so mankind can inherit what I gained. It means to stand in the bright claim Jesus is the gift to man that all need to find prosperity. I am the offering of value desired forth from the One who ordained me His own. The Master is the Creator of unity. Shallow hope is not a part of His character. We gain by reading the light of Scripture. In it is the written Word of faith. The Israelites are the examples of people God supports. Do they all tie to Christ? No, many have not found Him yet. But the future predicts it will happen. How do I know this will come forth? Scripture is always the truth of knowledge. It never has a false value. I am not the intellect guide for there is much for me to learn about what God has proclaimed but I invest in the unity it states. I believe the more I comprehend the farther along I will be when the time determined is before me. I grow with many who follow others in the way of teaching the light and placing it within the heart. To follow others who have value to the Bible is to stand on behalf of its supportive way. No one person has all the significance so read for yourself and gain the principles. You will know the importance of it and the truth will be within.

Structure to the heart is a gain in where the favor is found and gifted. The learning it takes to achieve a suturing of value may mean profound standing. To love the work, you've been given is to have the value of it within your heart. I am training to deliver so others have the hope I have been given. Does it require me to face the initiative of learning? All the implications of gain materialize where the heart is building. Scripture teaches the mind who the Living Word is. God is the manufacturing way of support. For He alone is the gateway to eternal hope. No other is the witness of unity. I know firsthand where to align my thought processes when I fear or lose confidence. I offer my stand to that of Jesus and in the way of it I hear Him correct my idea making. I do have the knowing aptitude it takes; action for good things to materialize but to serve in the way of faith one needs the beauty of God to align to Him in favor. I look at what my heart enjoys, and I know I am fed the unity of faith. In the way of working so others find the joining manner of faith I have the tie of God to me in a personal bond. Look to the work you do and invest so you can find the support of the One who made you. It takes the heart the hope and desire to perfect the work so others can hear the voice of reason. Instruction comes when a person applies himself to the forefront of aid. I have the work ethic of a powerful Being. He is my Creator. In His value system I know I am gifted ideas. I work to achieve them, so others too gain with character. Jesus knew the Israelite would not yearn for Him until the time of the tribulation era. Until this happens few have the courage to attain the verses of the New Testament as a witness to their spirit fed hope. I value the way others have given themselves to the mission field. I do not have the mission to do this in another region nonetheless to me the outreach for my county is supporting me. I learn while investing and in the work I do I offer to many online the opportunity to achieve in the same way. I have support for the one looking to pray and to be fed ideas of courage. I value my outreach, and I do this work to give others the will to achieve as I have. Does it mean I don't offer a goal for my own stand? No, I work for gain just as all of man does only my focal point is to marry man to God. It is the better hope and in it is the love of the One who secures man to His heart. God, the all-powerful Being, is my soldier of insight.

No one whose hope is in you will ever be put to shame, but they will be put to shame who are treacherous without excuse. Psalm 25:3 NIV

To know the One of all is character to Him with a heart of will procuring in the way of unity. True hope is bled forward where others learn and gain in the way of identity to the Living Word. I am not the saving way for I am merely a woman of favor yet, I believe in the true Word of the Most High. All have the option to gain if they so choose. Writing is one example of where one can contribute the light to another. Simple gestures are just as valuable. I am the unity as God is perfect within me. I am not the plan of salvation, but I lead others where to achieve it. I am supportive of the one who is in need, and I truly love the one who acclaims God is righteous. I am tied to the Waymaker and I believe He is good. In Him is the gift of life for it is recorded in the Book of Hope. Never has man been alone. Since the beginning of time God remained standing with courage and leading toward the people of faith. Adam failed as did Eve when tempted by Satan. We all would have succumbed to temptation as the craft of the enemy is to know us and how we operate but to have the Waymaker within means to have Him as our counselor. To learn where to find faith is a gift all can obtain. Knowing where to grant another this knowledge is a sight offered from on high. I tally no knowledge of whom I gained for this is not for me to know. Only God knows the details of my efforts. This, too, should be your idea of standing with Jesus. Giving should not hold the value of it in as far as record keeping. To give freely is what God values in His banking system. I witnessed those around me hold fast to their stand of wealth and little hope was bestowed. In turn had the gift been freely offered the reward would be great where heaven would know the sum of it. I look to where I offer my cash flow. Is it what rules my heart? Not in the way of banking for I lean toward the dream of sharing my God to others. That is where I hope to plant my returns. I must align to God for all my investing, and I do this with inspiration. Does this mean I never fail to assign all my gain to God the Father? At times I invest although other goals must be met. Bills climb forth so returns need to go to them as well. Is this in accordance with what the Bible declares? I believe it matters if you earn and offer your firstfruits to God, I also realize man fails at times in giving. Will this mean no fruit comes of it? It is for God alone to determine the value of our hearts and minds.

Christ, the focal point of men, is the unity of character necessary to thrive. I am not the all-knowing inspiration but due to the hope of God I am fed vibrant goal making. He hears me declare Him as holy and it brings Him closer to my heart. I invest where others are not willing so in view of God is support. To lead so others find the light is a goal I have where man and Christ can be united. Do I always have this in mind? At times I may lose focus, then it dissipates quickly. I value my God above all else and in this way, I stand on Him. The reason for my work is to secure others to God. I have the value of the Risen Waymaker and I place unity to Him. I am made of flesh and bone, so I will have negative thoughts, except they do not get fed. I work with hope and unity, so I am tied to the One of care. He supports my learning, and in His way, I find the faith to continue to produce. My work ethic is gold to the heart due to the study of Scripture. Both the Old and the New Testament make my heart gain. If not for the written unity I would be working for self. There is a better way to offer light than own selfish longings. It is represented in the offering from on high. The goal will never be that of individual lust or stained ideas for God is true and hope filled with character and good manners. He will not be a dark intent for He is only light. I thank Him for the faith and for the courage to press forth, so others hear the voice He portrays. My writing is this influence. He has provided me with gain, and I shall always tie it to His person. Storytelling is a gift and within it is a plan of hope if God is the focal point. To administer the favor, I have known is to align to God my goal making. I cherish this incentive. It is value beyond measure.

    I am not the innovative means to thrive for I am fallible. I walk where I am led and if it is to be that of hope I will know God is at work within me. I am attuned to share Biblical principles and insight. I do this in many forms. For me educating others to the call of God is far greater than to achieve a bachelor's degree for no gain of the spirit. Many prospered in where they did both. This is a blessed way to operate. I have the fortune of having others aid me where needed. I have the bulk of the ministry I do freelanced. Meaning I am not tied to it with debt. I am working in such a way that no debt is needed to offer my goals. It may develop into more and then I will need to claim a wage but I am working with the intent to acquire gain so I can build where I am called. I enjoy making a way for others to learn from. Does this mean classroom ideas are unfolding? No, I do not desire to stand as an instructor in the way of speaking instructions from a book. Experience has taught me I can offer my love of the One who made me by way of other means. I stand in the idea making and I look where I can operate. I do have unity to God, and I realize He, at times, has a different goal for me then I relate to in the given moment. I salute Him for the training He gifts, and I value Him even more when change happens. I know it will mean professing Him in faith and waiting on His ideas to flow. There may be others I need to bind toward, and the benefit may be that of hope instilled where loss once was. I have the united goal of tying my heart to His sleeve and to be standing with character. To value Him as the lead in my heart is a sure way of operating. I know my unity is valued and He will not push my hopes to the division line. He acts with pure love and in Him is the vested favor all need to thrive. The Israelites learned this when land was being conquered and

God supported them through the duration of the conquest. I, too, am not the only influence on the scene of the environment I work in. I know others care just as I do. Goals of favor arrive to the one who places his heart in God's way. The adjusting influence is far greater than one can fathom. I have known God to support me while changing my outlook to another stand but the whole investment was for the benefit of me and those I choose to serve. I am given support where I learn and in the way of it, I know unity is present.

The faith of a mustard seed can build into the plan of moral gain so all involved will prosper. I have the vision of owning a place of value where many find the beauty of God for themselves. The many recorded in history where truth was abundant were tied as the Israeli in that God was the focal point within them. I know from experience God moves where He is welcomed to. Where I labor is with the building of hope. If I do not see a plan where God is the center of what I am doing, I release it to the wind. God is the factor for my decision making. Lead where you invite Christ to witness your efforts. It will stand as character and favor for your train of witness making. I have the value of caring for many. I commissioned this way as gratitude to the King for He favored me with unity to do so. I know I would not act with faith were it not for my Caretaker, God on high! The redeeming quality of God is far greater to me than my own ability to act. I have the gift of sharing Christ, however, to know Him is far greater. I have seen many who believed they could operate on their own ideas. In this is self-reliance where no favor from God is given. They may have success only with no faith in Christ there is no reward. I know from the Word of the Lord He can build where I am not able. For this reason, I operate with hope. I know I relinquished my own goals for His, but it too, is good to do so. If you value the hope of God to your heart, realize He is the care one needs to prosper. I learn to achieve and in doing this action I have the knitted bond of integrity. God is the one who favored me with knowledge. In His value system I am fed unity. Is it for all time? I believe it will be as I have relational knowledge, He is the granter of it so I will lean into Him for support.

My support to the many who read my book material is a stand of gain I can relate to. If you're applying the Word of God to your knowledge bank you will ascertain my teaching is accurate. I know many fail to thrive due to no investment in Scripture. The Jewish nation is one example of people who stepped away from the prosperity of the written New Testament. Why this happened is due to deception. The Bible records when it happened and how it went forth. It is a unity in that it declares the truth in recorded hope. I know for certain God is who He claims to be. He cares for me daily and in Him is the knowledge I am His. The Book of favor is for all mankind to gain from. If it were hidden no unity would stand. To learn the Word and read the hope builds the mind a goal of support. I know I am tied to His character as I love His way of being. The shelter it provides is clear unity and in Him is the support I have a faith of true witnessing. The value of support is far above that of man's ability to aid. I labor to achieve the witness so many find the knowledge God has granted us to gain. I am not one to leave a conversation where God is being spoken of. If the idea of Him is good, we are tied in unity. If it presents as false, I know I am to witness the light so good favor can be had. Is this always easy? Not where hate is being seen. I will not hesitate to tell the truth of the Word, but I do not act out of haste. If bickering is all there is to be heard, I will walk away with no more incentive for man must determine on His own what he will engage in and how he will honor God. Some have the understanding they can operate with both the world's way and God's way. This is inaccurate. Only the witness of light will be recorded and having the value of the world will wash into the depth of no return. The reward to love God's care above man's knowledge is far greater than stating a love for the way of the lost. The message one gives is true or false. The yeast of the bread infiltrates the whole loaf. In the same way a false idea plant will lead to death. No person is complete until he realizes God is the one of insight. If you act with the idea God comes before the world you have grown in the way of support to Him. This is the work of the Most High. Know where to align Scripturally and stand in the unity of the King. It will bind to you in a gifted unity and holy walking will ensue.

The recording below is the Scripture reference where the Chief priests told the lie concerning Jesus' resurrection being false.

[12]When the chief priests met with the elders and devised a plan, they gave the soldiers a large sum of money. [13]They told them, "You are to say, 'His disciples came during the night and stole him away while we were asleep.' [14]If this report gets to the governor, we will satisfy

him and keep you out of trouble. "¹⁵So the soldiers took the money and did as they were instructed. And this story has been widely circulated among the Jews to this very day. Matthew 28:12-15 NIV

God supports the man who places his work in the palm of His hand. The Word of God is far above the way of man to himself. Look at where the Bible speaks of glory. It shall be gifted to God the Father not self. Man, dreams of being famous and having much wealth but when God is the implementation of the unity tying man to Christ the gift of recognition flows to the Creator. I am not one to achieve the merriment of standing on a platform and professing my own work. This is not what I choose to do. There are many who accomplished this with character. However, man normally pursues this for his own standing. I support the One who made me from the dirt and breathed life into me. Am I always right in this motion? I am fallible so no I don't always achieve this stand. I do work toward it where able. My influence is caring for those less fortunate. There is little I can do other than speak to the One who is righteous. I cannot make another believe or act with support. I learn as one who gains from Scripture and in the way of it, I know true love. Scripture is my mainframe. I adhere to the goal of sharing the light. I offer unity, and I enter into an agreement, so others learn as I have. Do I align to the great One of hope? Yes, due to the recognition of Him toward my person. I know to accept the will of God is to gift it toward another where able. I achieved this reward where many have also trodden. I look at the hope of God and import it to my heart. I have the work of God within and to place Him in the unity, care development means to progress with support. Find the bounty of God and be standing in the vested field management. I light the conversation around me with courage and I know I am secure with prosperity. I face the day with a stand of insight due to reading the true Book of hope.

Rich wealth is not for all men. Some find it burdensome while others work for minimum wage. The way we operate is for us to decide although serving others is for the believer who invests so another gains. I have the hope of leading so more knowledge can be had. I enter forward so man finds the value of the King. I do this to honor my Savior and to secure others to Him. Does it mean I fail at times in corresponding to those I meet? Yes, daily I must adhere to the One of great value. He is the way to eternal hope.

Many who lead find the value of Christ far above that of another. I am one who knows where the favor comes forth as true insight. I value the Waymaker and His stand of honorary timing. I may stumble and lose hope at times but when I entrust the One of hope memory reminds me who I serve. He is the influence of divine unity. There is no other who can complement me with character and trained mannerisms. I support the One who placed me in His care. I am providing the same to the many who read my book material. I am not the saving witness but one who knows where to find Him. I am intertwined in clear thinking due to the work of God within my heart. I am not simply standing on my own merit for God is the way of me. I am tied to His counsel and in the knowledge of Him I am offered the way to thrive. Support is a sight of good knowledge. To operate with character is wise and to share this knowledge is divine gain. I have the insight of sharing, so others learn as I have due to the work of the King in my leadership. I know it is Him who aligns me to His care for there is none so equipped who can maintain my heart. I have the hope of knowing Him so rich and so deep that we always act as one. Is this even possible? Man fails where God does not so no, at times I will lose my way. But to adjust my stand and claim my heart to God is the sole purpose I hold fast to. I act with confidence that the righteous way to know the Lord is to pursue Him in faith. This comes by way of Scripture and prayer. Both are vital to the recognition of Him. I have the gift of sharing this knowledge, so I plan on putting it in motion, so others gain as I have.

 My knowledge came by way of committed learning. I have been applying my heart to the Word of God for some time. I learn and prosper with integrity due to it. I am ever faith bearing to those in need. I do not have a following of great numbers yet; I know God can move swiftly if He chooses to. I work with ethic for the love of Christ. I am standing on the manner of His person. Faith is a part of my work ethic. If I fail it is due to my own understanding not that of the Lord's. Where the committed plan to offer hope faith is squarely present. Learning is a valued way of operating. To place the hope of the Father before men's hearts means to offer the plan of salvation forward. I have seen many who have not committed to following the great commission. Why is for them to discern. I work as though the people online are hearing my efforts. I am attuned to leading so there is a gift of inspiration. How this develops is from on high. I step toward the plan with character. In the way of Jesus man is fed. I proceed to the clearing of goal making so another has the heart of God to him. To know the many who gained is for God alone. In Him is the value of sharing light and complete good harmony. If none come with me still, I will work for them. It is for the man himself to decipher where he will gain. I know for me God is the ultimate way of favor. Leading is for the people who enter a covenant with the Lord in where they place the light to many. Why do some feel no gain in this action? This is due to a fake commitment. I learn due to applying the Word forward. Those without hope have no value to it. In the beginning there was the Word, and the Lord was in it. He is the measure of true hope. In Him is the beauty of saving. The light of character and honest insight is found favoring to those in need. If value is the quest know there is none more powerful than God. He is the stand of great unity. I speak to the one seeking to gain. I favor the willing with unity. To accept the light of God is to claim Him with insight. Scripture is the best way to know Him. I invite the love of God to me when I read it. Knowing the best method of planning comes in the way of knowing the One who made all things good. The digest of hope is favored from above. Leading is a value where all find the faith a reward. If you have chosen to reveal the light, you favored the path of true love.

Loving the One of inspiration is a way of commitment leading to an offered hope. Man alone is not a value in and of himself. Man needs the unity to God to be fed goals of achievement. No other than the Savior can bring to the heart a bounty of faith. In God is the committed truth so all find prosperity. I have the knowledge of the Word so an influence of support is within me. Do I guarantee the value is always going to be spoken? I am not the Almighty but one of His bride members. I can't know the finding of every incentive so I must too lean into God for support. The unity of God is a field of insight leading to a spring of truth. I have the invested way of the One who made heaven and earth so all the time I apply to Him is valued as good. I work to offer others the way of support by being in the plan of the Most High. He is an honor to me, and I gain in the way of true love. I know the work of God is always right and good. I do not have to invest without first believing in the One of great unity, so I never assume I am without His aid. To align to Him in support is to care about how I operate. Should the manner of hope be of a shallow hold I release it, so no harm comes before me. I stand in the recognized unity He is all-knowing. If I am called to attend to a means of action I try to invest in the way of light. I am not all-knowing so I will at times make a mistake in the decision arena. Does this mean I am without the hope of God when it happens? I believe God will carry me forward to the bounty I am to obtain, and I will not lose Him in the process. Knowing the saving ability of God is to offer it to another in need. I am committed to seeing where my invested time will be and how I will achieve the reward for the heart. I am never walking on thin air for God is the crafter of insight. Lead where you are given the opportunity and stay with the work of God, so you find heart goals above that of wealth of the pocketbook. In the work of it you will gain the respect and love of the Father. He is goal orientated and in Him is the bright way of faith. If you are looking to lead yet have no heart for people, you have no fruit to offer. Learn where the light is gifted and stand with the hope of God before you. It will represent the offer with care and a timing of beauty will blend forth. I know firsthand how difficult it can be to wait for a goal to prosper. I have the will of God within, so I am not immune to the way of Him. I realize His timing is not my own, so I look at Him with character. Lead with support and be granted the route of knowing how to perform so others gain a reputation of purpose. It will bleed to you a benefit in faith and guide one to the plan of Christ.

    Knowing the work ethic takes time and a stand of hope means to apply your spirit to the One who made all things right. I am never in the way of a loss for inventiveness. God moves and I intertwine with His character. We, together, work as a team. There are days when I feel overwhelmed or at a standstill yet, I know the One who made me His own is developing my way ahead. I have the growing aptitude to land with courage, so I inherit the gift of unity I am looking to witness. In the work of man comes the will to succeed. I have not the gift of foreseeing the future. Only the Creator knows these things. But where I place my heart is the plan of a committed stand that aligns with girth. I have no unity to a false recognition. It is not how I operate. I am glad to gift another where I am able but if darkness presents, I will not engage. I will walk on to a better insight. Leading is not for the thought process of only wealth in the pocketbook. One must work so another inspires forward the reward. I enter contracts when the truth of the people I look to bind to is presented. There must be a mutual knowledge of who the main idea is dedicated to. I am not the one to offer a lead before first understanding another's position. I know many will try to say they have Christ as their focus however, if the witness is not that of a guiding inspiration, I know it is not real. I am not the all-knowing God, so I must question and seek wise counsel before I combine my efforts with those, I hope to build an accord. I look at what the percentage is for something to have a foundation of hope. Many today follow the world and think they can obtain favor from God even though they work against Him. Simple voting says a great deal as to whether one is walking with the spirit of God. The invention of the telephone has made it an easy transfer of voices, although one must see beyond this to know how a person operates. The care of a partner needs to be supportive of the value of what Scripture states. It takes the will of the One who made all of mankind to be heard above the voice of longing just for the sake of wealth. I do know there are those who are quiet and not out in the mainstream view. I search for the most beneficial way to operate. If I get into a committed relationship, there must reside the knowledge of God and who He is to others. Simple questioning can bring to light where a person finds His thought process. I evaluate what is stated and I esteem where to apply my own interests. I know we must learn to expand but to go forward outside of the Word of Christ is to lose the hope of Him being within the operating budget. I am not the way to all things right and true for that is within God not me, however, I have the heart of Him working within me. I am tied to His way of thinking, and I endure for the love of His character.

There is the reward of sharing, so others gain, and in the ministry, it is often viewed as weak and unhealthy by the outsider. I have never regretted giving to those around me. God is true and in Him is the way of support. I now operate so others can have the witness of God to share. Do I ever fail in this effort? At times it happens. I am not the Waymaker so some find me offensive due to His way. I lead where welcomed. Am I to have favor either way? If God wills for me to gain it will happen. There are the many who believe if Christ is at work on your behalf, you will attain great riches. This is not written in the Word but to practice so wealth can be gained honestly is to operate in the way of light knowing God is the administrator of light. I am training to witness and in doing so I inherit the right to stand as a partner to love and hope. I am worthy to hear the Word as I am human, and God wrote the Book of hope for all of mankind. Do I feel the pressure to share? No, it is a welcoming way for me to do this. I am tied to the care of sharing God, and it feeds me with character. The many who slipped due to no knowledge weighs on me not due to my lack of merit but the fact I am not able to reach all of man. I look forward to teaching where I am gifted the opportunity and in doing this action others have found me as a friend. I am tied to the market of hope and in the beauty of it I am fed unity. To align with the goal of sharing the work of God to another is the spiritual lead I am a host to the Most High. Do I agree with Him on all things? I may have feelings of questioning, still I know what God has spoken is right and true. No one is perfect outside of Jesus. He is the one who viewed man worth the effort of dying so men could have life eternal. This matters to me more than all else. I invest where I am led and to believe God knows my witness is sure is a gift I have. The harmony of God is for man to have Him within his spirit. If you hear a voice drawing you to claim the King yet you stand away from the pull you will lose the connection more each time this happens. Without knowing the last claim to you don't risk the hope to wash away. The reward may never happen, and you will learn too late you lost the value of God and never invited Him within you. If this takes place you will have no hope of a birthright in where life after death is secure. Man is not tied to the reward until he determines to ask the Savior to his person. God aligns with the man who places his goal to Him to obtain the spiritual bond. Eternal hope is from on high. Jesus is the plan for man to prosper. Know the witness of true knowledge and be standing with hope for a committed union.

> [20]*But after he considered this, an angel of the Lord appeared to him in a dream. The angel said, "Joseph, son of David, do not be afraid to take Mary home as your wife, because what is conceived in her is from the Holy Spirit.* [21]*She will give birth to a son, and you are to give him the name Jesus, because he will save his people from their sins." Matthew 1:20-21 NIV*

God's character is for all of mankind to inherit the love He has and to offer Himself to the one who believes. Many achieve a way of thinking leading to dark developments. To take the viewpoint God is not caring is to say He is not vested to give love. But this doesn't mean you are to exploit the work you do. Shame is not the benefit of giving hope but with it comes the realization we may need counsel. In the Scriptures is the knowledge of how to operate and where to lead. We have the offered gain of knowing who is to stand with character when we recognize what they are saying. If it does not offer light, we know it is not of God. To know the hope God portrays we must read the Book of unity. If we fail to align to Christ, we will be swept into the current and fail to know the truth of hope. Bounty is not a reward if it goes against the Living Word. People today find it difficult to learn where hope resides. It is the significant way of leading provided in Scripture. If you press the envelope and have no stand of knowledge you are not the idea of Christ. In the making of favor comes the reward of knowing where to align. God is the only true Being of insight. There is no other more knowledgeable for only God can speak complete truth. I have the will to operate with God and to lead in His way yet, I am human, so I make mistakes. When this happens, I strive to correct the stand and make it right. I know the meaning of many is to perform for gain in the pocketbook. If this is your intent and you aren't willing to offer hope first, you are not tied to the great I Am. You learn to manage both the heart and the operating idea of Christ when you enter into agreement to His way. I have fallen where I offered no insight. It was a time of loss and pain. Once I determined to offer unity in the way of Christ I was restored. To endear the heart toward others is to offer the benefit of truth. It means to know the Scriptures and to reward your lifestyle with them. Operating with the idea you know what is best, although you aren't applying the light from God means you have no clear unity to Him. The reward of sharing the hope is to gain so others have the righteous knowledge found in the way of God. This is recorded in the Bible. Both the Old and the New Testament support the character of Christ. It matters where you read and how you achieve the gift of knowledge. If you think you are offering hope, consider what material you are transferring. Is the reflection of it worthy of God's hope? Can you share it without the contention from another who believes with a great commitment to Christ?

Think about who values what you share. Is it a reward to the one looking to gain knowledge of Jesus or is it your own understanding you are offering? There is wisdom to the one who knows he needs God and His teaching guidance.

Support is a need all of mankind has. It is tied to the way of sight known from on high. I have the hope many shall find the prosperity of God to their person. Does this transpire without man hearing the Gospel? God can share His own story by way of influence from Him. I believe not all converts heard the message from a person, rather that of Jesus in a vision or from His care to their hearts. I am favoring the work ethic of sharing the Scriptures for I know it means others are being informed by it. Do I support my own writing? Yes, for they are tied to the One of inspiration in holy committed standing. I learn from working and in the way of it, others are gifted the love I have found from God. I know I am not the unity Maker, but I achieved the knowledge by acting as a counselor of fruit. God is the gift to man I am merely a witness to this. I lead so man finds the same level of hope I have been gifted. Is there ever a dispute about my teachings? If I find an error, I am more than willing to change my correspondence for I know I am fallible. To learn is wise and in the making of the favor I am fed true knowledge. Share the light of your efforts and find the view a solid goal. I now have several writings online to gain the perspective of unity so stand with knowledge you too can achieve as I have. Your aptitude may not be to offer by way of writing or sharing with artwork. You have your own gifts that I do not; know to apply them toward the work of giving light is to declare Christ the way ahead. Little is the one who never places his ideas forward for then no achievements come into view. I have often had doubts of my own merit although today I stand in courage. A way to achieve means there must be the outright unity heard and administered. Leading is for all if they choose it to be.

My hope is for man to gain in the way I have found hope. To love the King and to apply Him to your sight of knowledge is to offer the goal of Him to others. I have seen man fail due to no unity to God. In the way of hope, one must believe God is the great Waymaker. Man is to align his heart to the Creator and to favor Him with his outreach. Know not all have fallen but many today do not envision the support God brings, and they fail to achieve the bounty of unity. I now know where to offer the light due to having been involved with Scripture and knowing its contents. I shall not remove this dream of sharing the hope of God for it is a plan of unity I engage toward. God, the One of beauty, is a knowing Being of opportunity. I believe through the power of Him we are given support. He never steps away if we seek Him with true honor. I am standing on the promise God views me as His child. I am not the lead of Him, but the work of my hand is for His name. Am I the reason another can know God? This may be what claims me the most. I know to give the Gospel to another is to offer the best hope available. I let God be the one to determine from there how things are to progress. If a person reads the Word yet has no value to it there will be no application of it to the spirit. I place my heart toward God, and I invest in His character, so I grow with unity to Him.

I am not the all-knowing One of inspiration for no other than God is the support we all need to exist. I look at where the value of my King resides. It is clear to my intent man will not fail where he respectively is always maintaining the unity. I have no fear of dying but I do not wish this. I know once I am in the presence of God, I will have eternal life. My heart will see Him, and I will be in His presence, and I will see clearly how to love all. Am I still yearning to gain recognition from Christ? I do not feel the need for He states man is His child. I know I am precious to God and in Him is the unity of sharing the work of Him. Do I have to adjust my schedule to do this? No, it is part of my everyday reward. Stand with the witness of knowing God is genuine and holy. It will become commonplace for you to offer others the love of God. I am one example of the many who have gone forth to acclaim God is the way to eternal glory. In the value of God is the committed hope we are tied as one. I shall not be in the way of no support for God is my Creator who loves me more than gold. He is the one who entered my spirit and made me justified. By way of sharing this insight I now stand as an operative who has the gift of prophecy.

The value of God is for mankind to have the gift of salvation. In the meaning is the idea man is tied to Christ. I have the gift of this within me. I hear the voice of the One who made mankind His own. Do you believe in the way of God as giving life sustaining goal making? I know from experience God is the one who made me alive and breathing. Without the promise of God there is no life eternal. You can manage on your own merit except where does it lead? I do the work of an author hoping for a following who learn the path I have been gifted. Is there a promise in this activity? God supports man when he offers his heart to Him. I value this as a goal of unity. I do not ascertain what my Lord will do with our commitment. In Him is the stand of heart acceptance and this I offer to Him. I know I am not the one to witness to the main stage of an arena. It is not for me to speak light to those from a stage setting. I value my privacy, and I am not interested in achieving the name of an actor or affiliate. But there are many who achieve a bright witness in doing so.

What sets apart the knowing from the lost is the message of insight being invited to the heart. God is this goal. I have the bounty of sharing the light and in the manner of insight I read Scripture to gain. For the purpose of sharing hope, one must work on his own unity to the Lord. This takes action in reading the Bible. This is how man thrives and gains a witness of hope. To apply the love value of the Most High work so you too have the inspiration of sharing light. I am not the author of all things good, although I do invest in knowing what is right concerning the Lord. It matters to me to divide the Word as it is written and not to add my own thought process to it. It is an insight into the heart where all is a stand of knowledge. The reward is a measure of pure hope and in the reading is the gain of knowledge that supports the heart and offers the mind care. I have known this unity since applying the Word to my person. Does it ever fail me? No, for it is holy and true. I may fail in the reading due to daydreaming or not paying attention; still the Word is consumed. I need the value of it for me to have the work to carry forth, so others learn. Do I do it for personal witnessing? Yes, I too am given the support needed to learn and apply love to my own understanding. Is the value of it more than spiritual? I have never lost hope when I read the truth. In the work I do I am vested to read and secure the will of God to me.

I know this happens when I gain the fruit for my own learning. I am not the only one who knows this is true for many write and offer the love of the One who made them. We all are given the option to perform for God. It is where our own idea making is placed that we invest and contribute. I know to learn the Word is vital to the witness I support. Love is the way to attain the goal of a witness who believes the Scriptures are valued. No other has the gain if he does not a stream, the light to another for in its presence sure knowledge is heard.

Gifted hope is for mankind to lavish on others in need. I know I have not always contributed to the work of man but today I invest where able. I stand when I need to share and in the way of faith, I work for others to learn. It has taken time for me to realize I am not the one to always attain the bounty. I spread my knowledge when it is deemed worthy to do so. When a person feeds my heart, I operate with support, yet if someone stands against me, I simply remove my efforts and let them choose their own way. I am not the great I Am, so I am not the one they are coming against. It is the way of mankind to believe what he chooses. If no attributes are seen, I know there is no value to God. I accept this as the way of many and in the knowledge, I am given grief. I do not dwell on the loss of others for it is not my call to do so. We are not the operating goal. God is the one who maintains the heart and in Him is the support we desire. I have no unity in the way of others if no hope is present. How do I know when someone is not working for the goodness of many? It is reflective in their outreach. If no hope is gifted, there is no insight to the love of the Creator.

I know mankind is often in need of sharing hope, yet it does not happen. It takes the heart the work of sharing to maintain the support when it is turned away. To shovel in the way of no outreach is to offer no value to man. I have the unity to realize one must move in the mixture of sharing, so others find the goal of hope for themselves. I invest where welcome, and I do try to share even when no offering is received. However, I do not force the issue for there is no benefit to do so. I learned I am not the golden view to man. The Gospel message is this hope. I value the way of operating so many find the support, but I do not have the gift of salvation. I can only witness there is this claim. I have grown in knowledge I do not have the path before me to align to all people. Even some family members don't recognize the truth of the Word. I am given the knowledge they may be known to God but the fact they do not offer others light is a way leading to no hope so what does it represent? I do not have the knowledge to one's heart and I do not need to know for God alone is the gateway to heaven. But to operate where no unity is given is a statement against the Lord not for Him. Do I join in when this happens? No, I say the truth of Scripture then I wait for God to work. I am not the way to thrive, but I know the One who is. I am intertwined in character to Him, and I love His mission for me. Will I know who calls to Him due to my efforts? No, yet I work just the same. For the light of God is far greater than to stand in the dark of no hope. I shall offer what I know when invited to do so but the hope of God is by Him alone. Many believe they have found the light when they operate against the King. Shall God not call to them too? I believe He does.

> *If my people, who are called by my name, will humble themselves. If they pray and seek my face and turn from their wicked ways, then will I hear from heaven and will forgive their sin and will heal their land.*
> *2 Chronicles 7:14 NIV*

The support of the One who made me is far greater than that of another. I have known the truth of this for some time. Where it came to me was due to accepting the gift of hope from my Savior. I have the goal of sharing due to applying the Word to my person. I learned the value of man and in the stand of sharing hope I unite to him. With the prosperity of sharing comes the honor of knowing God's favor. Does this look like the building process of no insight? No, for God above gifts us His knowledge when we place value to His Book of light. I am not the only one to learn where faith is built. If you look at the reading of hope you too will learn the meaning of insight. The gain will climb, and you will ascertain the heart of the gifted Savior. Will you know all there is to learn? No, for God alone is the one of insight to that degree. I am valued by Him for I am His. He calls me part of the bride. It is not a gest of no golden opportunity for in the way of the saving power of God man is fed unity. To hold fast to the Creator is to bind your spirit to Him with care. I learned not all choose to do this. But the one who offers the will of God to his heart is far more knowledgeable than the one who does not gain. I have the vested unity due to accepting the gift of hope and in the way of it I enter the throne hold of salvation. Do I make inheritable decisions based upon the work of the Lord? I achieve the best pattern I can. I look to God for my understanding of how to operate in a prayer ministry. I love to share the Word by way of involving others to operate with support to one another. It is a simple lead, so others too have a witness to guide from. Is there ever a doubt present? I am human so at times

I think about such things. But to learn to claim the right path is to engage in Scripture and support the work of it to another. I am not the goal but the one who shares the reward of it. I know many who can gift yet they choose to hold close their value system. Are they standing in direct contrast to Christ? I do not know the answer to this, still I maintain it is better to guide than to be without the influence going forward. I love the way of God for He invests to all the way of Him. His lead is wholesome and true. He does not play favorites; however, He does give favor. I operate so another can learn from me. I have the goal of gifting another the Lord's value. Is it the only mission I pursue? I have the talent of an author and in this field, I witness for God. It supports my character, and it stands as my desire. Should I believe there is a plan for me to offer in another form? Only God can determine where my steps shall lead. I have the expectation God will ordain my investments. He is ever faithful to provide. Is there a right way to witness? There are many who shared in prosperity outside of the traditional marketplace. I work where I am gifted as does all of mankind. Will there be a judgement where I fail to align to Christ? I endeavor for it not to happen. I work for the glory of God to be granted. Should I audit my own merit value? I let God determine where I am fed. I do have the unity to God, so He is ever able to perform on my behalf. Is it the unity I portray? God knows where my heart is drawn. In Him is the unity I value. Should I lean into another's viewpoint? If it is not Scripture based, I have no need for it. It is only a clang without a sound of hope.

Love from on high is a gift to the one who believes and invests to the character of God. The work I do is for another to gain and receive hope. Is this for all who believe in God? If you value, the love from God yet do not invest to another you are self-professing not light gifting. I am not the one to condemn someone for not influencing others to learn who the Creator is. But I do not believe someone who knows the Savior can stand at a distance and be intertwined with Him. For me there is only one way to operate when God is the focal point of the heart. He is more than a small detail to the day. My whole being is in love with His character. I have the heart of Him to share and in doing so I witness to the grace of Him to many. I am telling of His nature, and I proclaim Him eternal goodness. Would I ever fail to administer the value of Him? If I am not giving light, I am without hope so know if presented the option to gain in the way of insight I invest. God is the way to offer hope. It is through Him that my heart bleeds to know Him in a better way. This is due to reading Scripture and gaining the value to Him in this way. Knowing the value of care offered from above stands as a witness He is ever faithful. Belief is found in the claim of Christ not just the unity to Him. Does this mean you will always stand in a righteous way? Man is fallible. At times he will fail to support the Word. Are we all given to loss even though we know God is secure in Himself? I am not perfect, nor will I be until the time of my witness here on earth ends. I walk in faith, and I realize I have the hope of God within. It matters whether or not I operate with true knowledge or my own value system.

    I learn from the Book of insight. In the way of knowing how to proclaim the light comes the burden of giving hope with perfect harmony to God. You will not know God if you don't learn who He is and how He operates. I have taken the time to read the love of God and in doing this activity I share the truth I gain. I have knowledge due to the way of God working within me when Scripture is taught. To evaluate the Word as holy you shine forward and glory to God is given. Does this work for all of mankind? You know the hope of Him if you seek Him in care. I am always available to enter conversation with someone willing to learn who God is, however, I will not stand in a fight of no gain. Many aim to dissipate against the work of my authoring. This is not my idea of witnessing to support someone. I will not offer more intellect if the only outreach has been to cause strife and loss. There is no point to this activity. The way of sharing the hope is to align to God and view a stand in the way of faith. I tied my outlook to the way of God and in doing this option no forward loss ensues. I gain in the way of knowing who shares the Word for the love of the Creator or who chooses to disrupt the flow of the goal making.

    It is not necessary to follow all who read my work. There is no motive for this. I am not recording my own unity but that of the Savior to me. I offer the voice I learned and in this I witness to others. Do I always plan on giving what I gain to others? Where the Savior is involved, I hope to grant this hope to all. There is no other way to believe than to adore the people of God's heart. Many do not assimilate to the caregiving due to lack of study and no knowledge of God's character. Are these not going forth with a witness? I do not have the answer to this but to me it does not reveal one. Should I seek to learn where all have regard to Christ? I am not the offering of value. That honor belongs to the One who made you. Shoulder the line of defense and unite to the great undertaking of girth. It means to step forth and lean into others so they too can be given hope. To learn the value of God and not offer it forth is a loss to your own understanding.

    The reward of knowing the One of hope is to have the support of the King. I am one of His faithful followers. In Him I am fed unity. He cares for my needs and in the way of support I am not alone. Even though I may need something I have not been given this does not mean my Savior is without care. He stands in support of me, so I witness Him offer knowledge and gain. I may not truly be in the right situation to have the bond I hope to acquire. I know God is perfect in His judgement. He never fails a person. It may not seem this is true however, know God does not fail. He may have a different viewpoint than someone looking for a gain that does not provide value. I have the heart of sharing Scripture, but I am not the One of insight. That is Christ alone. To learn and guide is to believe the Father is true to His Son. I am one of the people who gained the inherit knowledge Jesus is the Waymaker. I am not the goal, but I lead to it. I shall make a way where I am given the ability to do so. But hope resides in the character of the Risen King. He alone is the main vein of our heartbeat. Know God is the care all need to thrive. I am ever in hopes of hearing how others found support from on high. I believe God is the Father of insight. To know the Creator is to gain in the manner of true witness making. It takes a plan of commitment for hope to build. Prayer is part of this offering. I shoulder the responsibility for my own path with God yet, I know He is the one I partner to. God is the Crafter of my heart. He leads me to the way of Him.

    I enjoy my outreach, though it is not the source of my unity. God alone is the value to this. In the way of sharing the hope comes the responsibility it must present with good intent. I know I am not all encompassing. I am built of more than spiritual guidance. Weakness is within me as with all human beings. I share what I am led to and in the knowledge of the Word I am given courage. I invite the work of God to be a part of my livelihood. Will I always stand on behalf of God? I hope this to be the way of my daily practice. I know not all time is valued by some as for dedication to ministry yet, a good portion of those who place God first realize to offer a good moral ethics system is wise. Leadership is not a loss rather standing so others gain from experience. I shall offer my intellect and provide what I learn so others too can inherit my offering of insight.

The mirror of God is far reaching and in Him we are fed unity. Do I know where all of mankind is going to be placed? I am not the unity to man, so I am not able to discern the role of humankind. I believe all who have the gift of support from Him will meet Him with courage and faith will be present. Is this all the Lord requires? He states for man to know Him he must believe in Him in a complete way. Not all who claim God is their Father know Him. They do not have Him within due to not accepting Him in a personal way. They will know when the time comes their support was not holy driven. I have the knowledge man is made from God's suture of life. I know from Genesis God made him from the dust of the earth. Do I know how this came to be? No, for I am just skin and flesh not the One of great knowledge. To gain so others are fed is a way of operating I lead with. Am I ever forsaken in my offered unity? God is ever faithful. It is I who fails in some respects, still God carries me through the market of faith. In Him I am tied to a secure reward He favors me as His own. I teach so others find this connected value. Have I lost my way in the sense of no understanding? I have made mistakes and lived in the style of loss, but I am not entering it now. I have a witness that seeds the heart with the voice of Christ. In Him is the support necessary to offer the lead of good care. I know I am tied to the Waymaker.

I have the role of sharing, and I claim the Word for my own gain. I believe I am given the lead of a voice in writing so others too may gain. In God is the unity to thrive. I am not the vested Caretaker for that is God alone. But due to His stand in my favor I am given the sight plan of knowing how to operate so others are fed true gain. Witnessing is not for the one who places no value on it. I have been standing in care, so others find the support I gained. Is this the only way to connect to another? Do you know another way? Is there a better path? No, to learn about the King is the only way to offer others light and faith. I am not the role lead in where my knowledge surpasses that of some, but I claim God for my own witness. This is declared by the One who made me His. I am not gifted in leading in any other route and I see clearly how to witness in this fashion. All the gold in the earth does not claim me for I am fed by the work of God. He shows me a path to offer insight, and I manage the work as a stand of insight. I have Scripture and through reading it I am given support. Do I believe I can conquer where another has not? My work ethic is for others to find prosperity. Does this look the same to me as it does to another? The one who places the value of God above that of a self-esteemed unity is the one who has the unity to Christ. I invite my friends and family into the nest of love by sharing my good viewpoint. However, some rejected my outreach and gone their own way. Will this tear apart our unity as a team? I am not the one to declare such things. Only God knows the true nature of a person's heart. Leading brings to the surface the way of God and in it is the plan of sharing the written knowledge. I too need to gain daily, so I read and offer the work of God to my spirit. No other is led without the purpose of sharing for God operates in the same field to all men. You have a wealth of opportunities to guide. It may not look like my ideas do but know God can build you in the way of great outreach if you are willing to offer it forward. In truth many find it labor some. I have not the fruit to gift without supporting those I encounter. Should I ever present a false faith? I have found the goal of God ever supportive, and I will always endeavor to maintain the will of God through this trust. Friendship is not always an easy path. At times it may appear to dissipate in where favor no longer builds. God is the one to always align to. In Him you can dream and find the faith of Him supporting you. Goals build and options come into view.

The LORD God formed the man from the dust of the ground and breathed into his nostrils the breath of life, and the man became a living being. Genesis 2:7 NIV

God is all-knowing and in Him is the fruit of life. Together with the Creator man is fed divine knowledge. We are tied to God in the spirit of faith. Many find the support a reward and they offer it forward. Is this the reconciliation man dreams of for future life in the way of heaven? You must know God and how to obtain His character to be with Him for all time. It means to believe and have the faith of a mustard seed. God is perfect and in Him is the work of grace. No person dead or alive has ever been able to secure his heart to God without believing in Christ. In the Old Testament we see where the faith is built. I am not suggesting no one from prior days has been gifted unity. I am sharing how God operated even then. He made it apparent man needed to know Him so He could be a witness to the way He operates. I am not the all-knowing way for I make mistakes, but I do have an abundance of knowledge due to reading the truth of God's character. The Old Testament is not one of no consequence. We need it for the foundation to be built upon. I have my work of my own insight, yet it is not the goal for me. I love the truth of God's care and in it is the support I find favoring. I have the will of God to offer another the insight of value found in the page material of the Bible. I am not small or in need; I am mighty due to my Father and His Son. I am secure knowing God is unity to me. I am fed the prosperity of share giving and in the way of it I enter to the heart of God. Jesus is the Waymaker. In Him is the gift of tying the work of Christ to mankind. I know the way to achieve and where to find the hope for it is written within my place of origin. God made me His own and I find Him glorious to know. He is my crafted bounty. Together we are one. I value His direction to me and in the manner of faith I am delighted to operate. I have custody of my mind yet, to align to God means to have Him with true hope. He is ever building me forth to a witness of faith. Should I work for any other? Why would I want to? There is no greater opportunity than to stand in the way of God's favor. I have the reward of knowing God is perfect. In His value system I am fed the knowledge He made me according to His goal set.

God is a factor of great unity. In Him is the idea that all of mankind is important. He created man to be a part of His family. He desired for all to know Him and to be fed from His hand. The Scripture Book of faith is for us to know how to acquire the important meaning to Him. He is valued when we read and, in unity, comes the main way to operate. In knowing Jesus, man is found favoring to life. Eternity holds the one who believes and who claims the Savior as his own. I am one such person. I have found an important way to acclaim the light and to put it in motion. In knowing where to align I have found the good favor of life. Eternal witnessing never fades. It is present where the heart breathes. I enjoy reaching others who too find the love of God fulfilling. If value is to be gained one needs to achieve the platform of true hope. In the way of sharing the offered faith one is set to adjust to the gift of insight. I have the knowledge God created me, and I am favored due to His love for me. I am not a single entity for there are many who know God. I am just a member of the body of Christ. I value all who know Him. I consider them my family. I look to God for hope and for the long-term relationship of insight. Growing in structure means I have been given the love of God and I claim it for myself. To know the One of hope is to gift it forward so others have the same benefit of wealth I learned. God works where welcomed. I have been standing in the way of hope for many years. God has not failed me once. I may have made mistakes in time though now I stand in a healthier way. I have a broken history, yet I do not dwell on it for salvation brings redemption. I learn while applying hope to my heart. This is for all of man to bear witness to. I am ever faith bearing and, in the Word, due to belief. If I miss time in studying, I lose my insight. This is not what I desire to be as. I accept I am not the One of great value yet, I am His so this makes me important. Structure is for the like-minded One of beauty. We have the committed hope of knowing where to offer light and in the offering, I am gifted love. Is there another profession that is more clearly uniting? No, I know firsthand there is nothing more precious. I love God and He shows me how to operate. I work with care, and I align to Him, so I am given support. Does He need me in His bounty? No, He has me as precious cargo. I love Him even more as He is not after me for riches or wealth of the pocketbook. I shelter others with clear expectations. This comes by way of sharing the light and stating its purpose. I have the gift of giving words and in them I communicate the vibrance of the Savior. He is ever bright and true. He does claim me as righteous due to Him not me. In the way of it I learned He cares more than any other possibly could.

Robin (Rochel) Arne

Unity Marker Five

The People of Israel are a Gift of Unity to Mankind

The glory of God is known to many. I can stand with the One of hope. I am leading in the book community and in the manner of faith I am built for endurance. To look toward God as my provider is wise and good. In Him I know I am made whole. I have the support of many, but God is the way to thrive and be given hope. In His value system I learn and develop options to prosperity. I now operate with true hope not that of self-reliance, but of a cherished knowledge God supports me. In the way of saying God is all-powerful I am offering the truth to others. I hear the hope of the one who believes and in him is the goal to align to Christ. I am ever being fed unity and in the growing I witness the value of God to my heart. Do I ever feel alone? At times I can, but this is due to my own loss of insight not that of God's spirit within me. To know where the line of defense resides, look to hope for the goal. In God is the manner of favor leading to unity and care. How do I support another when I lose my footing? I still know where to turn for the guiding hope to be shared. Even if I fail, I know God does not. I determine what is leading into the loss feeling and I apply the truth of Scripture to depart from the false value. God does not give one despair. In Him is the whole unity to gift one the faith needed to carry forward into battle.

Preparing of a book takes many ideas to form. I hear my Lord, and I recognize His lead. He acknowledges my presence, and we share the commitment of goal making. Do I lose my way at times when working and writing? Yes, it can happen, but it is not due to the One who made me. I am the one who is made of flesh. God is the great way to apply hope. Reading the lighted way guides me to gift another the hope I have been given. I yearn to know who has seen the light, but I am not the way so it will happen when

God releases to me the knowledge. Do I esteem to offer others the gift for the reward of praise? No, I am not standing on this way. It leads to loss and no gain. If you value the heart and have the notion you can align to the way of God prepare for your stand to be tested. God is not one to apply a false way, though Satan will do this to try to dissolution you. I have the hope of knowing who I made a difference in, but I do not seek to learn this avenue. I know God has it recorded, and I am merely doing His work of insight. I am not the one who determines who is given support in the way of faith or a petitioning of value. Only God knows the real reason someone is offering love or an invested way. I shall align to the care of God and lead with character knowing God is the gateway to eternal knowledge. In His value system I am tied.

The King is the creator of solid hope. In His way of presenting the light I now understand where to align my thought process. I share this gift freely and, in the work, I do many have the gift presented to them. I know no other is as glorious or holy. Only God is the gift of saving power. To value the light above the darkness is wise and true. If the heart yearns for songs of death or neglect it is not from on high. Even a simple county song can be a loss to the spirit. I am here as an example of one who has seen loss and turned from it. I used to listen to songs that broke the spirit. They were not uplifting, nor did they enter me with hope. They present as a connection though in truth they have no comfort. We look to entertainment with a value of hope. The truth of the world is not light. It stands as a negative and no support is gifted. I watched televised movies and was not engaged with the story line. Did I error in this? I am not without loss, but to align with a meter of negativity is a fall within the heart. I shall not always do the best for myself for I am flesh and bone. But to apply a stand of no intent means to commit no sin. I benefit from writing and in leading others to a plan of inspiration supporting the One of faith. I have the focus of God due to Scripture. No one can accomplish light without it. Death may proceed the one who chose to refrain from hope, but does it mean no benefit to heaven? Man is fallen and God sees the heart. If faith carries one to the heart of the Savior, much wealth is present. However, to wait to find there was no unity is a time of regret not insurance. Value your Maker and be committed to Him enough to learn His viewpoint.

There are reasons to commit to God and they hold value. There is not one negative thought to God that is true or just. For God is all things right and pure. Love is justified when God is the focal point. I am one who has lost in a marriage. Did I commit the ultimate sin? No, I did damage my own spiritual lead. I have not comprehension how damaged I am, still I know I am redeemed. God's support is gifted to the sinner. I value my outlook, and I share my story to secure for you the hope God does not reject you. He will offer you a way to know Him if you choose to. He never steps so far away you can't know Him personally. Each of us has committed numerous actions of hurt whether it was intentional or not. How it is deemed is in God's capable hands. I am not in fear of sharing the Gospel, however, I do wish I did more on behalf of God. Do I need to work to be given a gateway to heaven? No, it is for Jesus to carry the burden of this. Belief in Him declares He is righteous and true. For there is no better value than God Almighty. To love Him with an abandonment is to form a unity to Him with caregiving. I shall learn and prosper due to my quest for Him. You too can have the sight of hope. Be an administrator of prosperity and lead where many are in need. God will support you and hope will be granted.

The faith of the one who places his courage in the palm of God will be tied to Him with character. There are many who have no ability to discern the good way of Jesus. Should one not still offer the insight they have? I know from experience one may not know how to operate then stand in righteous ways once God works within him. I perform daily readings, so I stay connected to the Gateway of life. God to me is all-knowing and perfect so why would I ever leave this unity? I am not lost for I have direction within me. I care for those around me, and I offer the hope of my heart forward in faith. God is light and in Him is the will to perform in a righteous way. I am standing so others can inherit light and find the way forward for their own gift of unity. I am not the all-knowing Being of insight but to train under Him is sound giftedness. I believe I am of the favor of knowing where to align and how to witness. I operate so others can claim God for their own merit. To work to offer another the gift of salvation is to declare God the hope to man. In the value of Christ is the knowing way to gain. I stand on the promise we are tied to God spiritually. Am I the only way to hear of God? Heavens no! There are many who work to share the Gospel and who as I do commit to the offering of hope. I am given the support of writing and God is my mainframe. I shall not give a false way for there is no unity is doing so. I value my God far above any dollar stand. To work with care is to script the value of God to many. Share the unity and be guiding those who are less involved.

God is the unity tie we need to flourish. In the way of sharing hope man is given the unity by way of offering love to God. The need to gift another the love is favor to the heart. I know firsthand the light is a committed bond not one of no insight. God is a grant of insight man can harvest by way of support from Scripture. The stance of unity is for all who believe and work for a committed relationship. God is the one who maintains the heart. He is the unity we invest in. Do all achieve unity? Some will not believe so there is no root within them. Knowing the One of hope is a gift to the spirit. He ordains the person who professes to believe and who commits to Him with support. I have the hope of giving others the inclination to thrive by way of a committed hold to Christ. He is the reason to achieve. In Him is the goal to be had. The value of Christ is far greater than the ability to align to another. Unity is for the one who places value to God. If you teach another where to find the good of God, you witnessed the hope and planted it to another. Unity is for all so be vested and claim it as your stand of insight. God will prepare you to learn so you are given the respect of Him as a measure of faith.

Light is a gift from on high. The plan of God is for man to prosper and find support from Him. In the way of sharing this truth comes the call from the Father. Jesus is the one who made a way for man to know God. It was a seed of hope put into the heart of all. Know there are those who say there is no faith, yet they have not entered the unity found with care. To love the One of hope requires the spirit to embrace Him as his own. I know I am one of the many who has the unity needed to see God face-to-face. I have the hope of being raptured but I work for all to learn about the character of Christ while I wait. If the battle for the heart is till death reading the Book of hope is a necessity. The way of care is found within it. To love God enough to hear Him speak while engaged with reading is a gesture of unity. The care from God is favor. To know His way of being shines forth the bounty and the goal.

With the unity is the presence of Him. The Word is a sight of true inspiration. Share this reward and gain in the way of it. I have the referencing of knowing God is good. In the manner of Him is found support. He never leaves one to their own defenses unless He is asked to stay clear. He is a gentleman, so He won't force His way onto you. To view God with care is to claim Him in true honor. He is the force of reconning all need to achieve the way forward. God is superior to all. He never loses His step nor will He. The reward of Him is far greater than all the wealth of a pocketbook. Share the reward of Him and feed many. The love of God is strength. In His viewpoint we are given instruction. The Word of God is good for the spirit. It feeds it with hope and light. The spiritual connection is born, and faith is broadened. Knowing the value of care given is a sight plan formed by God. His way of teaching is the Book of insight. He instructs the heart and in the manner of guiding it never fails. To read the lighted Scriptures is a gain all need to witness by. The favor of God supports the work of one who believes and shares the honor of Him. To accept the light is to offer it to others. If you refuse to speak of God where is your faith being given? Are you offering it forward or are you presenting a false expression. God favors all who acclaim Him as righteous. It takes courage to say to another God is real to you. Glory to God is support to Him. When you offer Him forward this means you believe and witness He is important. Know God is fruit bearing. In His manner is unity of the mind. If your thought process is weak and there is little you offer another concerning Him where is your support? My witness is broad due to the way I choose to offer it. I am not on the hot seat, but I do say the truth in a public way. I run the risk of being attacked yet in the presence of God I am secure. Love is far reaching, and any can give this knowledge. How you present the light is in your court. Know God will receive your efforts and make them glory to Him. He is the One of good intentions. If you truly want to offer others the care of Him speak out and be not ashamed. God is glorious to know!

To know the love of the Creator means to believe in Him with your whole being. The way of sight is in Scripture and reading it brings to the heart true commitment. The love of God carries the heart in the path of guidance. God supports man where the love of Him is found. I know the love of God is genuine. I witnessed His work in me and have seen the outcome of faith.

The opportunity to share Him is far greater than any other investment I have been given. The support from Christ is far reaching. Man is the way to have a belief that can be false. The Word of Scripture is never a negative idea or instruction. I enjoy reaching into the congregation where church is being given and I align to the message preached when truth is offered. The reward of sharing the plan of God is for the one who is committed to Him with purpose. Knowing the real Creator is a gift and to believe He is your support beam is a secure investment. I have not always been motivated to gift others the Word though today it is a driving force in my heart. I evolved in the suture of God to me in a personal manner. I have the love of faith and in it is the solid support leading to gain.

Each person who believes God is the way to eternal witnessing is a beacon of inspiration. All people have talents. Some are made viable when action is given. Where the lead comes into play is the knowledge God is a sight birth of unity. Many find this as God filled knowledge in where faith is the support given. To know the real unity of God is a sight none can compare to. Each member of the church is not always in the right. Discrepancies can come into play where one person believes one thing and another something different. What stands as correct is what God declares in the Bible. Many are finding little knowledge is being taught. It is not the plan of God to change His demeaner. He will not conform to the world. Man does not have the wise gift of hope without the will of God within him. I know leading happens even when it is distorted so one must search for themselves the way to know God. He is ever present to correct the heart and mind when they fall into a path of negative influences. Support God and His unity and stand in a righteous way. It may bring others to the saving witness of His care.

> [15]*He who walks righteously, speaking what is right, who rejects gain from extortion and keeps his hand from accepting bribes, who stops his ears against plots of murder and shuts his eyes against contemplating evil.* [16]*This is the man who will dwell on the heights, whose refuge will be the mountain fortress. His bread will be supplied, and water will not fail him. Isaiah 33:15-16 NIV*

Scripture is for the one who places the value of it toward his heart. The better gift is to deem it all-powerful! The way to present the light is to care for those in need. Scripture casts light into any situation. Witness measures are given, and hope is gifted. The way of faith comes as well, and a garnering of love unfolds. To team with the Creator is to ascribe to the will of His hand. The author of knowledge is Jesus. He is all-knowing and mighty. To love who He is and how He operates is to declare Him your Saving partner. Many see mankind as weak and untrustworthy. God is the one who changes mankind's idea making. The unity to God is gold to the heart and in the way of it man finds prosperity. Love conquers the heart and professes a gain. Work for those in need and share the light you have been gifted. The all-knowing King can align your intake and make a gift of prepared unity. In Him is the idea of faith and it is real. To assure another you stand on his behalf is to offer a lead of intent. If you suggest a false lead, you cheated the person, and no unity will be met. You will operate with no heart of pure method making and God will not honor your output. Share with courage the favor of God and be a witness to His ideas. In the way of it a shoulder of hope will birth forth and favor will be abundant. Many today work for self-reliance. This means no insight from on high is granted. Do you connect to the One who made you whole? If so, you are a righteous person of favor. To support the love God holds is to ordain in His name who He is and how to know Him. The value of this is far reaching. Know no verse of faith goes into thin air. The work of God leads to man finding Him in a complete way. Invest in your neighbor and be hope bearing so he can find the faith you own. It comes by way of God not self. In the unity you will have the insight of true knowledge. God will work on your behalf and beauty will be present. Adjust your intake to meet God. It will be a sure method of inducing courage and faith.

So is my word that goes out from my mouth: It will not return to me empty. Isaiah 55:11 NIV

Light is for man not man for it. Why does it matter to share the Gospel message? God has made claim to Himself in this way. Do we question our own way and accept Him out of due process or for the value of knowing where to turn for hope? I have the idea God is all-knowing and in this knowledge is the sure way of faith. It comes when one applies his heart and mind to the Creator. In the sharing aspect of faith, one needs to attribute the will of God forth to another. Many neglect this opportunity. Do we esteem this as valued when we do not incorporate light to others? I have the acclaimed way of presenting gifts of insight by witnessing in the work of written material. Should I think it has no merit? This would be a false idea. I am not the tide to the water's edge, but I know where to share the force of it. All who believe in the One of unity know He is the great developer of insight. To say less than this is a negative. God is the support all need to acclaim Him as righteous. The light and care of God is an amazing thing to experience. The prepared way He operates is a holy commitment empowering the spirit to learn about truth. The shared experience of Him is gold to the heart. I am not the only one to learn of this great ability for man has known God for centuries. Adam and Eve were the first to meet Him in a personal manner. Had they not chosen to invite sin in they would have had a life of luxury, although all would make the same mistake as we have sin nature within us. No one would have stepped with perfect ways as only God is capable of this feat. Share the expectation of knowing the Creator and give the work of your heart the bounty. In doing this activity you will inherit the honor of God and His Son. I know them as my own for I place value on them, and I invite them within me. Both are one and the same yet separate. Both stand as one and acknowledge all of Scripture as good and formalized.

God is perfect and good. He is more than an artist of hope for He is the mighty one of unity. God's character is always good and true. In Him is the bounty and faith all need to accomplish the manner of favor to support another. The written work I do is not the only way to profess love to someone. Many are gifted in labor fields where they support with physical ability. Not all members of the body do the same gifted support. It is a beautiful thing to have the inherited goal of sharing light with someone. I value the hope I have found, and I mention it due to the character it breeds. To love the work of your heart is a plan of integrity that builds and unites with hope. People everywhere thrive under teachings from others. The work of God to the one who stands with support is sight where man is given labor and fruit comes of it. I shield the value with my whole being. I support the hope of God and in the way of sharing I am fed as well. Do many know where to offer light? I believe man does hear the voice of reason no matter how he professes. God is not one to forget any of His people. He works to gift man the will of Him. If you support God, the Father but are not inclined to offer Him to the one who needs His counsel you have no light stemming from your intent. Jesus is the plan of salvation and in Him is the support of gain. To value the work of others is a care all need to ascribe to. Share the burden for others and ignite the pattern of faith. You will abide in God and be standing with hope when the day of judgement happens. Unity is a sight of integrity too. It claims the heart the pattern of faith and in it is revealed the gold of God to the spirit. Love is an entanglement of faith. The party who supports light is never in the way of loss. The unity of God is far above all of mankind yet, this is what God chose for us to be as. To witness for care is a solid goal man needs to achieve. In it is the atoning way of spirit led favor. There is no other way to achieve this than to abide in the Savior and claim Him as good.

The hope of mankind is found in the gift of salvation from on high. Those who proclaim the gift for their own way are wise and receive favor. The fruit of the spirit is from the Lord. Jesus is the welcome One of hope. The unity of Him is for man to have a connection to Him in a personal way. The hope of God came from the heart of Christ. Do all need to hear the Gospel message? I believe God uses mankind to offer the work of Him to many. The mission field is far and broad. The inspiration of sharing the light is a unity given in support and favor. The way to give another this gain is to stand in courage and offer the lead of the Savior. Do all who find God hear this intent? If you focus on God, you will align to Him and know He is the way to better follow the value. It is real to those who have the belief of Him within. The all-knowing way of God is for man to align to His character. The support of God is for many. It is not obtained by imposing self-indulgences to another. That is not the way to thrive or share a witness. The hope of God is for those who are witnesses to His caregiving. A word of a soft-spoken preacher can guide man or lead him astray. In the knowing capacity of support man is given the unity of Christ but the truth of Him needs to bear witness in harmony to His character. The measure of faith one has is not determined by the amount of his bank account. God supports the one who places the heart in the palm of His hand. You must be standing in conjunction with the Creator.

Power can happen in where Satan has a claim on someone however, there is no value to it. Money means no tame control without God as its source. The unity of Christ is far greater than wealth of the hand. The exact knowledge of God comes from Him. His record is within the heart of man, but it needs to be developed. Man has the choice to offer himself to God or to refrain from Him. But when judgment comes all will admit God is genuine. The truth of the way is written in the codebook of insight. Is it a mystery to man? Know it takes the accepting of God for the unity to be there otherwise you read and learn head knowledge. The spirit is the connected value to God. It is set apart from the role of leading. In it is the character needed to offer the truth of God to others. To bear hope for another you must first know the way to it. Stand with the One of great value. In Him is the first light to gain. There is no greater value than God. He is the way to eternal wealth and harmony. The work of man is not significant in where he labors for no hope. Only God can deliver the faith that cements the work of His call.

Christ is ever present in the believer. In His counsel man finds the gift of salvation and it blesses his spirit with support. To know the Creator is a gift of a fragrance in the spiritual sense. To travel the world with no hope would carry one into the realm of knowing no partner. The lighted path defines the Maker and in Him is the gift of hope. To gain the light but have no option to learn where to place the value is a small entanglement of insight fleeting in nature. The unity happens by way of Scripture reading. God supports the unity and in Him we are fed true gain. The value to God is a stand of unity. Should one not invite the care of God to his heart he will lose the idea and the more he negates the advice the less value it has to him. This is dangerous and should be left to the wind. The unity is a sight where man faces the longevity of good faith. To believe in God yet not support His viewpoint is not a wise path to follow. Where does it lead? Only the Creator knows this answer, and I would rather look to truth than express a false value. Today many follow the lead of no influence from on high yet profess God is their King. How can this be? I do not redeem so it is not for me to say, but for me to align with God is the wise decision to pursue. God forgives the man who repents and says he is sorry for acting out of character. I know I have made poor choices only now I am walking by sight not self. It is a better formula to be engaged in. Witness the value of God by knowing where His viewpoint originates. Anyone can give an idea of his own value, but it may not join to God's stand. Would you desire a faith bearing person to share a message you aren't on board with? I wouldn't. In the scope of God, He is far above my knowledge. He hears the heart and what it contemplates. The value to His way is better understood when the application of truth is gifted. The better heart bond comes by written knowledge and care of hope. Read the plan of salvation and know God is mighty to redeem. The battle for your life depends upon it!

Review John 3:16 once more. It is the valued Scripture of true knowledge. In the way of support, it is gifted to the one in need of more clarity. I yearn for the way of God to my heart. In Him is the measure of favor I have been given. I am fed by His caregiving and in Him I have unity. The faith I receive is for the man who places his being in the palm of Christ. God is ever faith bearing so work to know Him in a personal way. Read the Book of hope and share Him so others too gain His favor. I know the work I do makes a way for others to learn the saving way of God. Do I have the gift of sharing due to the acquired way of support from on high? I believe I have been showered with faith for the intent of enlightening those who desire to gain. To love the One of insight is to stand in the faith and bear witness to His way. He is ever faithful and true. Do I know this for certain? Yes, for God has been righteous with my heart. He has granted me the work I love and in doing this acclaimed support I too gain a stand of hope. I embrace the love of God and in Him I am tied to His caregiving. He never fails nor does He align to a negative way. He is gifted, whole and pure. In Him I stand with clear intent and divine hope. Should I act out of haste and spend time advancing for the sake of opportunity for the pocketbook? I do not operate with this in mind. What I do is portray the work with the hope of enlightening others to the call of God for their unity to be given. If I fail to align to God, it is not due to His misstep but that of my own for He is always surefooted. Leading is for any who say they are committed to the value of God for the goodness of Him to be gifted. God works in caregiving and in Him I have support. I lead so another can claim the King for themselves. I invite the work of many to gift the plan of salvation forward. God is the way for this to be. Know any of His supporters are given the path to perform for Him in a personal way. Lead so another has the gift of support and tie your intent to on high. You will know the way to gift unity and glory shall be given to Christ.

How good and pleasant it is when brothers live together in unity! Psalm 133:1 NIV

Glory is found with the good work of the King shining into the mind. The care from God is for the love to be shared. Know God is for man and not only the created Being of insight. The love of God is far reaching. It offers the knowing a way to prosper. Lead so another hears the love God has and be given over to hope. I know many favored the One who made them. The battle for standing in a partnership is ever enlightening when God is the one you act in accordance with. Unity is above the work of no heart value. God ordains the spirit and in Him is the way to prosperity. Leading shines when God is the focal point. It means to invest in the union and share the bright way of giving love. Hear where the plan of salvation originated. It came from God not that of man's influence. It is part of the building one needs to invest in. There are many who favored the light and claimed it as good. Yet many have no stand to its call. Why this is I do not know. As for me and my house, we will serve the Lord. The call came to me as a child, and I believed wholeheartedly in the equation. God the Father is the owner of my intent and Jesus is the Lamb I serve. Together we work as a partnership in the way we operate. Do I ever stumble and lose my way?

Man cannot be completely given over to no sin. Not until the gateway to heaven has been granted for man has the nature of sin within him. God gave us the choice of whether to turn from it or to engage. There are many deceived due to the pull of it. The world embraces the lie it holds as an attraction worth supporting. This is false. To believe in something other than the Savior is a false idea. God is the way to life eternal. Man may divest in this goal but if he doesn't stand with the unity to God there is no light within him. Have you seen and heard of hope yet been without it? It is due to no accounting of where the light is captured. I know I am not the only person to have failed in my walk with the Lord. All of man has sinned at some point but for me to gift my story is not a draw. I prefer to tell of the glory of my Savior. He is the reason to write and tell of the spiritual way to life eternal. In Him is the true work of a witness of love. He is far more in tune to my feelings and hopes than I will ever be yet, He does not override my goal making. He places my stand in the path of good intent, so I know where I am to step and place my value system. I am not one to offer no fruit. It matters to me where I gain and how I attribute my knowledge. I share the love of God so others too can gift mankind the harmony of hope. To use my book material or to write a note concerning my expressionism means to be offering the light in a forward way. Leadership is not the height of my heart, although it is the manner of faith I work with. God is the way to achieve a plan and how to grow it forth into accomplishment. I stand in the manner God has gifted me to. I look to God for a way ahead and in Him I have the opportunity to produce care. This has meaning to me as a person of faith. Support is a sight plan from on high. The gift of sharing God is birth to my spirit. I know He works within me and trains my heart to offer the unity I gained. Does it come easy to say God is supportive to me. Currently, it is not difficult to do so. There may be a moment where I hesitate if I am being pressured in some way, however, I know that is where my faith is abundant. God is the Shepherd, and I am His child bride.

To secure for many the love of the One who made him is a solid hope put forth to the mind. The goal of sharing the light is far reaching and is standing in harmony. The gift of knowing who made you is glorious to the heart. In the manner of support man finds the knowledge of his Caregiver. The vibrant way of the Scriptures to enlighten is a garnering of hope for the mind. The care never fades and in the way of it all strive to learn. In the corporate lead man must work to gift another a path to learning how to maintain the corporation as the entity to support them financially. The work of man is for many to have the lead of the sharing, so others find prosperity to the pocket. This is not the ultimate reason for working. The path to clear hope is not just for money to be had. The unity to God is based on a spiritual guide not that of insight to the pocketbook. No one ever hoped to acclaim the support of the dollar without knowing it cost them a part of their work ethic to achieve. The many who tout it as the only reason to achieve have lost the value of it. Money has a purpose where it can shower one with hope in the way of gain for knowing where to apply it. To operate with the reward as the only means to align is a false idea. Man places his own witness toward what he finds valuable. A lead is for the one working to claim a goal of importance. The true love of man is from on high not from what he gains financially. God supports both the worker of insight and the one who shares the spirit of Him to another. I am not one to align to the fame or the glory of importance, but I do hope to point to God with a major tie. Do they work together? This is in the power of God's hands. I do not know the way He plans to align my favor but to me to stand on behalf of His name is a gain none can compare to. Work is not for the weary of no insight. It takes stamina and courage to continue where others failed. Strive to share a simple goal and watch it blossom forward.

The knit unity of Christ is intent in the way of favor. God supports the one who offers his goal of leading. Whether one stands with care or determines to operate in the negative God is the way to learn and be vested. If you are achieving the goal of unity without the knowledge of who made you align to the work ethic, you have no hope of gaining the support from on high. Your pocketbook may prosper yet where does that leave you on judgment day? If you are working to gift others the lead you have found the reason to apply effort. The work ethic is what matters to Christ. You don't have to have a corporation tied to you for there to be unity. Work in the way of true hope and apply your best efforts to the work ethic. In the way of sharing faith, you will offer love, and a growing ability will be seen. To adjust your station of support to others is to care and align to God. He cares more for your heart than the reward of wealth to the pocket. Is there a way to have both? Practice the work ethic of sharing light and God will build you forward. He is good and true so know He will align you in such a way that your abilities will thrive. This will result in future goal making. Where it stands will be to capture the many in need who come your way. Time vested is wise and good favor is the seed to the plant.

God supports the one who places value to His way. The man who places hope to another is a plant of inspiration. The goal being light to another. If the value of God is within you then prayer plays a role in your life. To offer the knowledge of this is good harmony. Teach man to align in the way of speaking to God through the communication of hearts. It means a better formula to the heart. The mind is vested when prayer is in play. The lead is not lost, and the true value is witnessed. Prayer is for the one who places value to the King. In leading one must pursue the goal of hope. It is no different when caring for God. He values time with Him in the communication field. The love of God is far above the average stand of fellowship. God is perfect and good. When you offer your heart to Him in the study of sharing your ideas God works to grant the gift to you. You must be aligned to Him with character. Leading is not a small thing where no value is recorded. I have the faith of a fellow believer and in this I am made righteous. Why has God ordained this type of unity? He is the one man needs to know to be granted the value of hope and its eternal witness. To operate with no value to Him is a stand in the negative way. Shower your heart with His counsel and be guided to offer love forward. I share due to the many ways God has prospered my love to Him. He never leaves me without inspiration. He is the vested partner I hold fast to.

Leading comes into play where man is fed the gain of His character. I am not without a level of hope for God knows my every need. In His value system I am given the support of the heart. Do I ever fear? At times I can have a notion of this except when I remember who my Lord is I gain in respect to Him. He is all-powerful so there is no reason to fear man. Man can harm the body, but he can't obtain the heart. God is the true love I labor to claim. In Him is the reward of true hope. I have been devastated in the form of placing more value on man than God. This was poor judgement on my behalf. Rest in the love of the King and know Him in a personal way. You will inherit the faith and in the goal of Him you will gain favor. God is not one to offer a false stand so if you are in the workings of something outside of faith you are not in His will. Return to His way of being present and know He is ever within earshot of your partnering. To know the way to work is a gift and the manner of it speaks to the one who prays with unity when faith is supportive to him. I am not one to lead without first asking God what His intent is. If I have no understanding, I wait for the discernment to be witnessed. God is not the negative influence man can be. Guard your heart and know the way to thrive is more than an investment of no importance. Those that know have the sight birth of reading Scripture so the mind is taken to the heights of heaven.

In the giftedness of sharing light comes the bounty of knowing hope has been given. Is there a way to always know what God has determined for you? One must operate as though God is in the mixture of the investment, but the appeal must be according to His favor. If you are tying your heart to something not of value according to God's way release it to the wind. You will be better for it and the true care God has in mind will come into play. Work is never a loss if God is the focal point. Lead where the door is opened and adjust your thinking to the One who made you as you are knowing His call to you is supportive. The investment will abound, and true favor will enter the heart. Grow with the love God provides and stand with support. You will inherit the lead, and growth will occur where unity is broad, and faith is given.

The Scripture of knowing how to operate is favor to the heart. God builds where He is invited to do so. The unity of His care is found to be written in the page material. The all-knowing lead of God is far more than a simplistic novel of storytelling. It is far greater to know God's heart than to offer your own idea of love to those you meet. The reward of sharing the light is a grant in the mind. God is the support man needs to flourish. In Him is the steadfast bounty of a gift of meaning. I have the knowledge God created the whole planet and all the stars above us. Do you see how mighty He is to man? The Word is the appealing draw man finds value in. If you invest in reading the hope filled log of heart knowledge, you are a witness to the good it offers. Share the hope of the Scripture base and be maintained in harmony of the heart. The unity of the Caregiver is for man to have the gain and for him to learn the true nature of the King. God is the mighty reason to offer others the Word. To believe in the One who made you is a support means of unity leading to gain in the spiritual sense. I am not one to align to the derivative of no gain. It is far better to invest in the lead of God and His way of being. Christ is the measure of support necessary to arrive to the witness He is just. The speaking of man does not offer the true witness we need to learn by. I am not the way to life eternal, but I know how to find it.

Therefore, I invest in those seeking to learn the true nature of a righteous Lord. The beauty of knowing where to gain is a plan of hope standing with character. I am ever faithful in how I offer my unity to God. He has ordained me to believe in Him and I enjoy leading others to the throne of His heart.

To know the King and align to Him is valuable and good. Not all are willing to know God or His claim to them. Will this stand for all time? I do not have the answer to this question, but God Himself knows the whole of the way. In Him is the salutation of good character. I am not the way to thrive, but God is the reason I look at others with hope. Man can be a challenge in many forms. Knowing the way to offer light is a plan of work declaring the love of Christ to others. God knows the offering I give. In Him I have support and good leading.

The commitment of the One who made all mankind is for eternity. There is no advantage to losing faith. When one operates so many have the promise of God before them is to ascertain light toward another. In the making of hope is the stand God created it to bridge the work and tie it to Him. God favors the heart where the support resides. To know God is the one who makes a heart thrive is to offer this unity to man. In the beginning of faith, one is fed milk. As time carries forward hope builds, and unity is created. It requires the heart to invest in the manner of Christ. This takes the application of reading the Book of insight. You never have to yearn for more knowledge if you read Scripture each day and learn from it. Favor is an important gain from God. He gifts it to the many who claim Him as their own. To learn the Word and to be gifted to the love from the Creator is to purchase the faith in the commitment of trust. I value the One who calls me His own. He is ever faithful to me in a personal way. I write for others to learn this knowledge. It carries to the one who purchases my writing works. Do I have to know who has witnessed by it? No, I am not the reason for advancement in the faith. It is God alone who offers the beauty of care and unity. He is the way to have abundant gifts in the spirit filled way. I am not vested to align with this process, but I do have the ability to share the Word which is a spiritual plan.

To know the King and to align with Him is the way to have knowledge and offer it to another. I am not one to train in the classroom setting. It does not call to my heart. I am remote in my location, so this too is reason to operate in a different manner. I care for the one who does have the gift of spreading knowledge in the classroom. I am partnered to this goal with support. God leads the math equation of His building formula and in the manner of knowing where to spread the knowledge is the tie of a committed unity. Each person is given the value of God, and it is what makes us unique. If you have the idea of sharing light God is working on your behalf to do so. He never invades the mind, nor will He lengthen the stand if it is not for a good fruit gain. The timing of God is not our own. We must realize God has the answer to every problem. If you are a witness to the love God offers you have the knowing aptitude, He is genuine and good. The lead of Christ far surpasses man's intent. Pursue the faith of God and invite Him to lead your heart. A unity will blossom, and hope will be given. True love is the mainframe of God. In His value system is insight and goal making. Accept the lead from on high and be committed to the length of the trial. You will learn much by way of instruction in favor. God tempts no one. Faith is a part of the experience. Build with a hope in care and be gifted the way to tie to God with support. It will mean faith is being had.

Now faith is being sure of what we hope for and certain of what we do not see. Hebrews 11:1 NIV

Christ is the one we need to have faith and love toward. He cares about all of mankind. He feeds the spirit with a vocation in where favor is bestowed. Man is not a simplistic being. He is multifaceted. His work is a gift when the heart engages with progression. The work of man is for all in need. We require a profession in order for a witness to be had. To pay for our own keep we need labor forces. I know many work at a computer and this is where they achieve the monetary wage necessary to thrive. I am one example of work being tied to the computer age. I have not the intent to learn a new profession however, I do hope to have an establishment where I offer faith support to those who come for an idea in faith. Will this happen? I do not have the knowledge of it. I can only implement the gifts I know to give. Whether God is willing for me to achieve this stand is for Him alone to discern. I work as though His way is before me. I have the gift of the heart in where I love to witness to those who come before me. I work with this goal. I am not the limited being of no hope yet, I know without the Lord's aid this will not occur. Should I fail, it will be due to me not the Waymaker. I realize God may have a path leading to something other than what I envision. This I stay committed to. I wish to work with the King not against Him. The holy way of God is far greater than my knowledge. I lean into the possibility of my dream happening yet, it is not my focal point. I let God determine the way of it. Should it happen in a different manner I will support it. I believe God is sufficient and in Him is the care and support best suited to my endeavors. Leading is for all who stand with courage. I have the support of my own gain, but I know God is far better to partner with than not. Should I lose my unity for the love of something I am not equipped to have? Never would I hope for such a thing! God is my focal point. He is the reason I live and breathe. I am not the gift of unity, but I know where to find it. This is the means I present.

    To know the One of great value is to offer it to others for the sake of good for them. The unity to God is a stand in where faith is abundant. Knowing the Lord brings to the heart a unity and a guiding hope of inspiration. Love conquers hate where truth is revealed. Man is not one to offer insight until he has understood the way of Christ. He is the perfect plan for mankind. To know Him is a foundation in where the lead is all-encompassed. God's care supports the one who believes and does not let the outside manner inflict loss. To know God is to care for those around you. The unity tie is far reaching and in its path is righteous gain. God supports the man who places the faith into action. Share the love of God and know Him in a personal way. To align to God is for the one committed to Him as Savior. Jesus is the birth of man into the light. Care is found where the truth is present. Have you been given the value of something yet not known how to offer it to others? God portrays the way and in Him is the stand of insight. Faith is broad and true where the love of God is present. In the interim of favor is the true work of the One who designed the hope. Many have the gift of giving though not the will to do so. If you value, the offered care from on high it will be gifted to others as it feeds you with support. You won't be afraid to gift it to another as the hope will be transparent and forthright. God leads to align mankind to Him in a personal way. Scripture teaches us to gift one another the value of Christ so good work will be had. The way to thrive is to declare the hope eternal in that God is all-knowing and just. In Him is the fruit of life leading to the manner of knowing where to operate. Favor is found by the one who applies his goal to God.

    Adjust the framework of your heart and tie it to the accord of Christ. You will inherit the unity and both you and God will align. True hope is built where the One of insight is favoring you. Know the lighted path is broad where one can find support. God is not secretive. He expresses the goal of a good partnership and in Him is the unity to have abundant gain. But know the pathway is narrow to receive Him. Jesus is the only way to have success in the spirit. The faith of one who places the wise goal of hope is the man who has found the necessary birthright to eternal unity. God, the Waymaker, is always at work. He never sleeps nor slumbers. He is in control of the heart and its stand of opportunity.

Where does one learn how to gain in the way of eternal glory? He accepts the invitation from the Jew called Jesus Christ of Nazareth. Knowing the Bible is a good seasoning of insight. Leading so others hear the hope is also an invested path of goodness. Biblical knowledge is not a simplistic find it is one of all-encompassing gain. God is the power man needs to find a witness of standing. If you have respect yet no heart faith where will your offered hope come from? God is the way to place forward the beauty of Him to others. It must seem to some a farfetched goal. Knowing the Creator is a gift of acceptance and not one of sole custody to the heart. You must believe in the gateway called Christ. It is an example of faith one must invite to his person. Would man have an option greater than this? What could it be? God alone is the gateway to thrive and have hope. In His value system is the knowledge of who He is and how to know Him. Biblical gain brings this forth. To love the written Book of faith is a measure of favor from above yet, it is man who must reach to claim it.

God's outreach to the one who believes is solid and good. The way to gift another the love is to apply the heart toward him in faith. How does this look if no one is willing to ascertain the way ahead? God alleviates this and moves on behalf of the heart. He incorporates the unity and gives man the will to stand in conjunction to Him. Hearts are not made of clay, rather a spirit-filled hope resides. It comes to the field of gain when it believes God is who He claims to be. Allow the will of God to act on your behalf and recognize His lead when He presents it. The way to adjust to the path is favor from on high. The knowing will claim the birthright and offer it forward. Suturing happens and goals become the draw in where to know the King is foremost within the heart and mind. The many who claim God have not all known Him in a personal way. It takes dedication and instruction to have Him within you. Reading Scripture invites God to your heartbeat. In the main way of favor is built the love and idea of God. Within the heart is the pleasure He gifts and the growing way of Him to your stand. God is perfect and good. He is the value of the great Waymaker. It is Him who stands in perfect harmony with your spirit. You can't believe if you refuse to invite Him within you. His care supports the love value spoken of in the Word. He manages the heart and reveals to it a better pathway. To have the unity to God without the acceptance of Him is not applicable in a life, for the true Word of God is alive and ever faith bearing to the heart.

The light of man is not the same as Christ's eternal witness. In Him is the glory of one who maintains the heart. Man offers love in a defined way not admitting a problem in weakness. God is far above this! In His way is the measure of faith needed to carry the heart to a plan of beauty. Not all people believe God is all-knowing. They find this idea weak or not of value yet, in truth they know it is true. Share the love of a true manner and gain the knowing unity it gifts. God supports the lead of the one who claims Him as his own source of vital favor. In the way of support God never fails. He is the care and the ladder of inspiration. You climb to a height where knowledge is gifted to the mind. To believe in the power of God is to align to Him in true gifted ways. The value of God is leading man to know Him in a better way. He is not one to offer faith in something yet, not bestow the way forward. To learn where to gift some with unity is to offer insight found from Scripture otherwise it means little to those you put forth a witness to. God is the way to offer upright gain. In Him is the gift of salvation which means no loss will ascribe to the heart.

The shield of faith is a given if one obtains the level of hope valued to God alone. He is the Waymaker and in Him is the plan of faith none can compare to. To shadow the work of another is to claim it for future development. The way of God to prosper man is to record to him the gift of His counsel. God is the one who made man so in Him is the unity as well. We need to affirm the true nature to those who are looking to gain in respect to wealth of the heart. It takes the will of a caregiver for others to find hope from another. It will be a gentle offering and in the way of it will be true committed unity. God is the only way to achieve this. He is the value of all combined in one Being. No person no matter how famous or given to teaching can reward others as Christ is able. The salvation gift came by way of death on the cross. It meant bloodshed had to happen, but it had to be that of purity. God has the will to carve out the plan of hope with care and unity to the heart. In the way of sharing the knowledge man spreads the light and carries it in the process to the mind. Glory is vested and the manner of knowing the character of God comes the sight plan of His way. Should man believe he can grow as much as God is able to? No, for only God the Creator can work in such a way. He builds with true unity in where we offer our hearts and minds His way of being. His representation is knowledge and truth. It comes from scripture, the gift of hope He provided. All through time God crafted the Word to be shared. He mastered it through His people. It is inspired by His holy way. Build with this hope and know you are united in the goal.

God is brilliant and true to those who love and cherish Him as their Creator. In the way of knowing the Savior man is fed support of the heart. The value reaches the spirit and in it is the gain of merit. Christ the King is our mentor. In Him is the way to align to the Father. They are one in unity. Both have a separate way of being yet, they are tied as one. Is this known to the people who have no value to Christ? No, for they do not worship Him with true honor. God desired for man to have a way to know Him. The blood of Jesus is superior to any other thing. We know this is the case as man has no offered ability to alleviate the stain of sin from him. Only Christ's blood does this. We invest in Him if we truly love and honor Him. The man who does not accept Him as his personal Savior loses the unity He portrays. Many feel as though to love the Father is the only way to be present to Him in person at the judgment seat. This is false training. To unite to the Gateway is a sure principle to achieve. Knowing the way to offer hope is a plan in and of its own value. God speaks to all of mankind. He leads man to Him. He does not stain the heart as the enemy does. Satan wishes to cause one to miss the hope and to have no value to the One of might. Jesus is this way! Light is found in the care of Christ. Its value is far reaching with no end to it. In the a.m. man is found at the throne if he prays but true is the same of the p.m. The work of God never fades or loses unity.

Our Father is solid to mankind. He, however, knew man would not claim Him as His own without a reason to serve Him in a just way. Knowing where to aspire is a sight and to lead in the same manner is support. God does this with care. In Him is the unity portraying light. The witness of God is far above that of all else. To believe in the One who determined man would have to believe He is good is the stand of hope God enlists to all. The Gateway is the great and mighty Lord! He claimed man as His child. In the value of it comes the reason to offer hope. The nearness of Christ is within the people who know Him personally. He is the Gatekeeper where all may have eternal riches. To place your heart in the hand of God is a far better method to life than to bleach white the offering with no way of being seen as good. Sin is wiped away when the blood is applied. It takes the heart a committed favor to God for this to happen. The way of sight is found in the efforts of man to gift another the love of God. Sharing the Gospel is the way to define your knowledge. God is all-powerful. He does not need man to act on His behalf yet, He made the term of our hope based on His sweet bond. Sharing this unity is well intended. People who offer the light are never without unity for it is within them. Knowing the plan of the ministry God provided is a solid gift in the way of spreading a sure thing to others. The witness of knowing who the gain supports is a party affiliation of good harmony. The belief God is all good stands as the true idea of who He is. The manner of sharing can be a simple method or an in-depth one. It is tied to the doorways that present. Should one offer their building ability for free? To speak to others in care is wise. But the mission field has many operatives who make a wage. Both act as a combined favor to those in need.

The just way of God to operate for many is a favor all can attribute to Him. He gifts the heart the knowing way to proceed in any endeavor. God is right and good. To Him we are His people. He works so we can achieve the best way forward. Value to Him is in the way we profess Him as the Savior. When God is our mainstream of hope all ideas build with care. If you are training to acclaim a new field of study work on behalf of God's spiritual leading. You will learn how to grow and where to contribute the light. Many find it lucrative to stand in the height of a vested gain and they bind to the idea rather than the Creator. This is not the way to stand in faith. God knows the one who offers the return of hope and in him He will grant favor. The love of Christ is viewed as righteous so know to determine to lead with Him as the focus of your goal means to believe in Him with character. To be someone of intent with God as the focal point will gift the many who come forth to witness your objective. God is the way to attribute Him in faith. It is by His leadership we witness His achievements and count them as His mission for us to complete. The way of finding where God desires for you to work is not a loss it is rather a unity to His person. Leading is for the imaginative. God supports those who work with the purpose of sharing Him. It is the reason to achieve and build in good standing. Any business entity can do this type of administering. Even if it is concrete being poured if the light is being offered the knowledge is shared. I have the reward of hearing the Lord and what He has to offer me. At times I may struggle though when I am patient, I become available to God. He may work in a slow manner, or a swift gain may occur. What matters is how I present to others His unity. God's light is seen in the man who places his will toward Him. The luck of man is not realistic. It takes effort and planning for the goal to be achieved. Endearing rewards come when man accepts, he is not all-knowing. God is the spiritual lead one needs to claim the bright way forward. The fruit of God is tied to the goal of His counsel. Lead with expectation and guard your heart with care. God is the one to invest with. He does not desire wealth of the pocketbook but to tithe is an invested unity to Him.

A tithe of everything from the land, whether grain from the soil or fruit from the trees, belongs to the LORD; it is holy to the LORD. Leviticus 27:30 NIV

Glory is a gift to Christ where it is equated to Him with faith. He supports the work of the one who witnesses His character. Know if you are working to declare God is holy you are on the path to success. God incorporates the way to prosper. He gifts the man who claims Him as His Savior. Knowing the lighted way means to believe and pursue the King with hope. God is not one to offer a false incentive. He is valued by the way He operates. To know the manner of Him is to stand in courage and be tied to Him with care. He is incorporated in the way He aligns to mankind. He bears forth the value of Him to the heart. In the unity man adheres to the will of God and he aligns to His way of being. Share the way of light and be written in the lamb's book of productivity. Is it where man finds eternal life altering hope? God is the one who gifts man the way ahead. It is the salvation way of God to offer Himself to those who choose Him. Will man ever find this for himself? All the people who offered their hearts to the King have eternal hope. For He is not one to misguide the mind to something false. Know the where withal of God is and be a witness to Him with pure goal making. Leading is a requirement when new ideas are being built. Not all have the inclination to offer a plan of insight if God has not placed it within them. He offers the will of His call where He is welcomed. The beauty of knowing God is superior means to achieve the hope of Him for oneself. The reward of God is within reach. Be vested and thrive with the meaning of insight being granted to your spirit. God does not fail the person willing to claim Him as Savior. He will develop and plan and make it grow. It may take time and an investment, but the gain will be achieved where it is supposed to. Know God values the work of Him, so others unify to His person. If you have the stand of sharing Christ, be atoned in knowing God will work on your behalf. Righteous unity is for man when he believes in the power from on high. God supports the work of the one who maintains the light and professes it to another. In the reward will be a tie of hope reaching the highest level of inspiration. God offers value in where man is fed unity. To know the way to attain this bounty is a stand in where the light is profound. Grow your knowledge and gain in the way of faith. It will benefit you with trust and the spirit of you will enhance.

God is perfect with love for all of mankind. In His value system is growth and opportunity. The unity of His heart feeds the work man does leading to gain in the way of instructive care. The prospering have learned where the faith brings them. The support of God is far more valued than any other. To perform so another has the capable way of favor is to offer a plan of support. The way to gift others goal making is to share the support you gained. God is the Waymaker and in Him is the unity derived from Him alone. To speak to others where the learning comes from is to align to them with character. The gift of sharing the light is a goal many achieved and gained. The Scripture I know feeds me and I learn as a result. To witness the whole Bible is solid in its favor. I read through it many times yet; it constantly enhances my heart. I know it takes endurance to continue to read the Book of Light. Man often feels why bother but to know the unity from it is gain. The ability to engage with care for the knowing of others is true hope cast forth. I have the support from on high and I stand with courage as a result. Many have the will to offer hope but no bounty as to how to proceed. It takes the knowing will of God's care for this to thrive. Share the way and feel the gain as the love flows forward from your heart. To invite the Scripture work to your entire being is a solid goal of insight. The value of God is that of an instilled unity that can't be matched in some other form. To believe and invite Christ to you is unity declaring Him your Waymaker. In the way of support God is perfect and given to perfect leading. The source of a writer comes to him when God moves in his pathway. I have the heart of God, and I place value to Him above all else. He gave me the way to provide enduring standing so others can build with care too. I have been in the swamp, and I will not look there for future enlightening. It was a time of brokenness, and it was fear that drove me. Today I have the commitment of favor, and I see more clearly how God operates. He remains with a person no matter what is transpiring around him. To know God as my Savior has brought to me the favor of His guiding. He is real and He knows how to lead. I care as He does, and this has made me righteous and giving. To teach another about the witness I learned is a goal of hope I lean into. God supports my offered way, and He gifts me the unity I need to flourish. I thank Him for my favor and in Him I am rewarded.

The love of God is far more than any other being can offer. Unity is that of much wealth. Man is for the better of the earth. God desired for man to know Him in a clear and unified way. Support stands as a right and good offering from on high. God alone is the one who determines the plan for each of us. How we work is based on whether we believe in Him and that He works for our best interests. To love God yet, not apply Him in a forthright way is to place your own idea upon Him. God is unity and good character. He values the way we operate and who we focus upon. If others are our concern, we are working to establish the best possible intent to many. We have the gift of knowing what our hearts are vested in. Man is the one who says what he will build to. The levelness of a plumb wall will determine whether the foundation is built correctly though if the ground has not been worked as it should have been nothing will keep it standing rightly. God focuses on our heart and what we relate as good. If we are working to inherit the money alone, we miss the option of hope for another. Our banking is not always that of hope bearing influences. To seek God and put Him in play before another breeds light to many. I know I offer hope due to reading the Book of Aid. It expresses the better path, and I follow it. Have the courage to offer hope and watch as God offers it to those who claim Him as their own. He is good and true, never with losses. God will offer those you meet a bonus of instructive care when you align to Him in faith. Does this mean preaching had to happen? God works with comfort, and He can ordain the simplest of offerings. To know God has character is to believe He will ordain your intent and make it stand in support to Him. Where there resides the love of God also is the means to share Him. The Bible records man as having the stain of sin within him. This is where man must acclaim the truth, he needs Jesus to be cleansed. God made man to have fellowship with. We are His guide in where we teach as He has taught us. The goal should be to align to Him in favor not loss.

The knitting of favor from on high is a gift of support needing no accounting of your own merit. God is the true way of it. In the manner of knowing the lead of Jesus comes the value placed upon the death of Him at Calvary. The record is clear and supportive of all. The gift itself is ever bright. It will not fade into loss. God is acclaiming to man He is ever faithful. In the guiding of Him is the care of the One who places hope into man. Where the favor resides, man is fed. If you feel like there is no point to reading the Book of hope you are without the pull from God. Know you can invest in Him and retain His goal of you with caregiving. The study of the Scriptures brings to the heart the retaining virtue of the King. He is always the sight to pursue. In Him resides the hope needed to flourish and grow. I am not one to offer no value now that God is my reason for living. It is His way that precedes my own thought process. I am ever thinking of Him. He is the fruit I need to have the ability to live. In Him is the glory of the gateway to life ever after in good will. He leads so man can have the retention of His name. God is the unity feature all need to have support. He maintains the heart and calls it to Him. We can either invest in Him or walk away but it will mean either hope instilled or no fruit to the heart. The more we believe and apply the insight the better we enrich one to another. To have the gift of knowing where to find the spiritual lead is a growth in care.

The light of God comes into play where it is welcomed. The unity provided is for the one who places his heart in the palm of the Lord's. Knowing God is righteous and good. The acceptance of His way is bounty to the one who has found the gift welcoming. Leading is for the one who sees clearly where to offer hope. It will flourish and grow in a meaningful way. To believe yet not implore the heart with the work of God is to remain at a standstill with no foundational guiding. God is the lead to man. In Him is the good way of unity which gives the heart the faith needed to trust and obey. God supports the one who places his hand in the right location which is His palm. Love is the guiding way from on high. Jesus is the gateway for life ever after in good and meaning filled character. To believe God has chosen you as His own is a solid way to operate. In Him is the incentive to offer this same way of presenting to many. The work of ministry is the body of people who have the will to share God to another. We have the offered way when we place faith into action. God is bright and good with a lead of instinct none can compare to. Invite Him into your life and be given the support needed to prepare for all others a virtue of favor. God will gift you the way and know He will not tempt you into a false environment where no hope is given. God is the way to be with courage and hope. He is the delight to man and in Him is the way of favor.

God supports the way of a committed partner who believes in Him with his whole heart. Would you invest where the root is not developed? In the gift of knowing the Savior is the tie to Him meeting the will of His stand. To know and believe the saving power of God is right and true means to have the heart of Him within you. The work of God is far above that of man's ability. The garnered way of a committed hope is for the willing to learn from. God works with character. In Him is the faith to bestow and place forth to all who call upon Him with hope. God is the factor of relief man desires to have. The work of one who plans to offer a good bounty is the sound investment of insight. Leading is planned and in the growth comes the goal and the offer of light. God respects the one who prepares the favor of a unity and makes it stand with good teaming. The way to gift others the prepared knowledge is to offer the Book of hope. The Bible is the gateway to know the reason for all the efforts to be applied. If you value the Word of God but are not committed to searching for the knowledge a growth will not occur. You need to be vested to learning it. The enlightened know the meaning of reading for the value of it not the wish for fame or monetary reward. The value of God is for the one who places his heart in the mainstream of the work. The belief God is the way of hope is to have the unity tying the manner of his heart to Him. Leadership means to have the gift of managing talent although the one who has the heart of God leading him toward the faith of Christ is a stand of insight. Knowing God, the One who developed the earth and the stars, is to have the best influence one can claim.

The fear of man is not a stand to believe upon. The knowing way to operate is to believe your Caretaker will align with you for good unity. In Him is the goal to flourish and find faith abundant. He is ever faithful to the one of hope. He provides the knowing ability to have the courage to apply effort and to make the goal be secure. Tying to the Gateway is wise and good. He will ever provide favor when you are living for His way. The present stand of your idea may need a corrective measure so look for the way of it to be clear. If you have the faith of one who places his ownership to God, you are working for the correct unity. The value of knowing your Lord is the complete package of faith. Look to the many in the verse of the Bible to be secure in how Christ works. He does not change or lose His way. In Him is the sufficient way of support so all concerned have the favor of Him. He ties man to His person, so gifts of opportunity abound. Look at the course of action supporting your endeavor, and you will have the knowledge of whether God is working for you or against you. It takes patience to offer others the light. It may happen in a quiet setting or in the brightness of sharing with all. God knows you better than your own heart does. He will not advance into harm. He will perform so faith is abundant, and you are committed to Him first. The real advantage to working with God is to have Him in your corner for all the trials and longing that happen. He does not go against the heart. He instills it toward His way of livelihood. The battlefield is not one of flesh but of desires. In the way of knowing who the reward is and where to find Him is the placement of Christ to you. Know God is ever with you on your quest for life.

"Be strong and courageous. Do not be afraid or terrified because of them, for the LORD your God goes with you; he will never leave you nor forsake you." Deuteronomy 31:6 NIV

Glory is for the One who places His hand upon mankind. Yet, with the care of God can be a sound investment where you are shining in front of people. The love of God is far above that of wealth but when favor comes into play rewards follow. God works with those who prefer Him over all else. He enacts the path of hope and builds with structured love. In Him is the value we share. God supports the man who has the influence of others. Where God is present good things form. The unity of Christ is far greater than any other thing or person. The belief of Christ's care is a stand in where man is solid and true. This only takes form with God as the focal point. Man alone has no value to him. He is weak and without a pure way. God perforated the spirit and sought a clean slate to be washed by His blood and made righteous. God is the influence we must embrace, or a negative will abide within. Righteous work feeds the man willing to learn and embrace the leading of God. The value of saving a person from death is a hope God offers. He is the offering we need to have a life of eternal good leading. When God is our target maker, we gift others what we learn. To share the work of God brings a reward better than any other investment. God is perfect and good. He leads with the will of a mighty gain. In Him we are tied to the unity He presents yet; we are our own entity. That is why man choses for himself who he will follow. Support is an idea from on high. We need others to be able to obtain a bounty where all our minds' gifts flourish. Without the love of the Father man is lost. In the unity of building so another finds prosperity is the creative measure of God. He makes unity thrive and hope fulfilled. To bend to the offering of the One who created you is to gain in the way of all things good. The abundant way God perforates the heart is the call He offers to learn and develop good intentions. The desire of man is to succeed. He hopes for wealth and good rewards. God permits us to plan and to push forward to gain only know the way you offer hope is what stands connected to the One of importance.

The committed way of operating is a solid unity where God is the guide. In the way of sharing the hope is the gift of salvation. It is far greater than man can comprehend. The goal of God is for all to know Him in a personal way. The light He provides is far reaching and faith is put into action when it is received. Faith is the guiding dignity all claim. Where God is the focus man is fed upright intent. The knowing will gain a stand of importance, and the brilliance of God will burst forth into a blossoming unity. God will ordain the commitment and truth will be abundant. Righteous goals will exude the knowing gift, and the preparedness of favor will pour forth. Lead with courage and trust God to partner with you. He will advise you and show the plan for a definitive faith to be spread. Glue holds man to God, and it is powerful! He will not fail the heart, nor will He walk away from you. He is good to the core so know you have a friend in Him.

> *14 You are my friends if you do what I command. 15 I no longer call you servants, because a servant does not know his master's business. Instead, I called you friends, for everything I learned from my Father I made known to you. 16You did not choose me, but I chose you and appointed you to go and bear fruit, fruit that will last. John 15:14-16*

Robin (Rochel) Arne

AUTHOR BIO

    Robin is an artist who shares the love she possesses forward. The gift of writing is secure, and she portrays the love of the Father through her work. Her residence is a remote farm site with her spouse who substantiates her goal of being an author and an artist of clay. She plans her day around her Savior and He is foremost with her. The light from Him is shining at her side and she believes He is the one providing for her daily. Her intake of Scripture is abundant, and it speaks with hope to her heart. The way of favor is not slight due to the gift of study she upholds. Talents have brought forward many attributes and she works for them to shine on behalf of Christ. The faith from His hand pours into her. She loves the remote life and prefers to be planting in the quiet way of spiritual guiding. Her aspirations include owning a facility where she offers the love of Scripture in the form of artwork and written material she has created. The love bond to God will never fade and she has taken steps to secure this action for all time.

advbookstore.com

www.ingramcontent.com/pod-product-compliance
Lightning Source LLC
Chambersburg PA
CBHW060528090426
42735CB00011B/2412